# THE WORLD'S GREATEST
# ROCK 'n' ROLL
# SCANDALS

# THE WORLD'S GREATEST ROCK 'n' ROLL SCANDALS

**DAVID CAVANAGH**

OCTOPUS BOOKS

Published in 1989 by Octopus Books Limited
Michelin House, 81 Fulham Road,
London SW3 6RB

First published in 1989
ISBN 0 7064 38787

Typeset by
Rowland Phototypesetting Limited
Bury St Edmunds, Suffolk
Printed in Great Britain at
The Bath Press Limited, Avon

# Contents

# SEX and...

Robert Plant of Led Zeppelin

# Led Zeppelin

'Led Zeppelin', Jimmy Page once said, 'is a stag party that never ends.' If ever a band was born to party until one or all of its participants keeled over it was Zeppelin – a rocking, rolling, careering orgy spiced with stories of black magic rituals, shotgun weddings and wakes.

Page was the frail former child prodigy guitarist who put Led Zeppelin together after his band, The Yardbirds, fell apart in 1968. Linking up with session bassist John Paul Jones and a brace of Midland neanderthals, Robert Plant on vocals and drummer John 'Bonzo' Bonham, he set about re-interpreting the delta blues in a hard rock context. Zeppelin played at deafening volumes to record-breaking audiences. For a while in the Seventies they were outselling The Rolling Stones at the ratio of three albums to one.

Through all this success they made merry, causing all sorts of astonishing rumours of backstage perversions to reverberate round Europe and America. Tales of massive orgies with willing female participants abounded.

The two stories that began to circulate like dogs on acid during their first American tour in 1969 (the Brits had rejected them as blues pilferers without talent or finesse) were sordid and thrilling, respectively.

The first was that never in the history of human conflict had so much semen been implanted in so many by so few.

They were in essence the groupie's Godsend. Two of them – fresh out of the Midland murk, not too knowledgeable but willing to learn; the other two – wise-ass London musicians worldly and cynical enough to indulge in the eagerly-proffered bodies of young America.

The other rumour had its roots in probably the most baffling phenomenon in the history of blues music. It concerned Robert Johnson, a young Mississippi blues singer and guitarist in the years leading up to the Second World War. Johnson had left his hometown as a fairly unconvincing talent, and certainly no genius, and returned almost a year to the day later as a possessed, electrified magician. Those who had known him were in no doubt. In accordance with the beliefs of the time, Johnson had sat down by the crossroads on a moonless night, met with the Devil himself and sold his soul in return for money and fame. He prospered for a while, wringing songs of magnificent tortured splendour like '32-20 Blues' and 'Love In Vain' from his occupied soul. But attempts in 1938 to locate him and put him on a national radio show proved fruitless. Johnson had been murdered by a jealous husband, struck down by poison tantalizingly on the lip of fame.

Jimmy Page was known to be fascinated by Satanism. He was an authority on Aleister Crowley, the Great Beast, 666, the English Beelzebub, the

Wickedest Man In The World. His interest in the occult seemed more informed than that of a mere dilettante. Obsessed by Crowley, the eccentric mountaineer-turned-mystic who strived for a plateau of sexual and narcotic gratification, Page went so far as to purchase Crowley's former temple, Boleskine House, overlooking Loch Ness. This was a brooding, sinister place, reputedly haunted by the ghost of a man who had been beheaded there. In 1970 Page became laird of Boleskine. The king of the colossal riff was putting in his bid for magus status.

Right from the off, everything about Zeppelin spelled big. From their sound, a Page-produced holocaust of guitars and drums, to their gargantuan manager, Peter Grant, to the hordes of dazed and confused Quaalude-guzzling teenagers who patronized the band, to their own appetites for more, more, more, Zeppelin went further than any band had dared to go.

They picked up widespread notoriety on their second American tour for an incident in Seattle in which a groupie was allegedly battered about her naked body with a dead shark, before having pieces of it inserted into every available orifice. Their former road manager, a libertarian karate-expert named Richard Cole, whose thirst if anything exceeded that of his charges, explains what really happened:

'The true shark story was that it wasn't even a shark. It was a red snapper and the chick happened to be a fucking red-headed broad with a ginger pussy, and that is the truth. Bonzo was in the room but I did it. And she loved it. It was like, "You'd like a bit of fucking, eh? Let's see how your red snapper likes this red snapper!" That was it. It was the nose of the fish, and that girl must have come 20 times.'

Later on that same tour they were joined by a journalist named Ellen Sander, who was filing a report for *Life* magazine. She wasn't to know it but a book had been opened on which of the entourage would bed her first. When she left the tour she went to say goodbye. She was almost raped in the dressing-room, only the unexpected chivalry of Peter Grant saving her at the last moment. She did not write the story at the time, but later she wrote a barbed account of life with the 'animals'.

Page's attitude towards women has remained shadowy. As liberal as the others where groupies were concerned, he nevertheless used Cole as his go-between. A likely target would be informed that Mr Page would be interested in making her further acquaintance. On one occasion Page joined the rest of the band in erotic contemplation as one of the famous Plastercasters was gang-banged in a tub of warm baked beans.

Referring once again to Crowley he said, 'Crowley didn't have a very high opinion of women and I don't think he was wrong.'

In 1972 he began a long affair with a 14-year-old American model, Lori Maddox.

'You'd hear a lot,' she says, 'about Jimmy being a sorcerer or wizard and like that. I think he's got a lot of power in his own little way. Sometimes when we were making love and it had been going on for *hours*, it was like being in a magic spell.'

Crowley had developed the knack of 'sex magick', the prolonging of the sexual act, delaying orgasm indefinitely to produce a drug-like trance.

The other members of Led Zeppelin were finding exciting uses for their hotel rooms. At the Tokyo Hilton Richard Cole and John Bonham sliced their rooms to shreds with samurai swords. In a Nantes hotel Robert Plant was informed that there was no milk on the premises. In retribution two floors were flooded with fire hoses and the toilets were jammed.

They soon found out that the best fun could be had from launching huge hotel televisions out of top-floor windows and watching them smash in balls of blue electric flame on the street below. Or, at conveniently coastal hotels, by throwing them into the sea. Once John Paul Jones took a TV apart and glued it back together again in expert fashion – on the ceiling.

The inspiration behind this mayhem, and quite often the violence that resulted, was John Bonham. Bonham was an awesome drinker who missed his wife and family. On the Zeppelin private plane, Starship, he made a hopeless attempt to molest one of the stewardesses. Richard Cole pulled him off and calmed the girl down, and then told the assembled gentlemen of the music press that not one word of the incident was to reach their news desks.

Bonham became so chronic an alcoholic that a doctor had to be brought on tour to look after his bowels. If they travelled by road the vehicle had to have an in-built toilet.

He also had a deep mistrust of the press. While Page laughed off the bad reviews Bonham could not understand why Zeppelin were not universally acclaimed. Approached one night in a Los Angeles bar by a writer from *Sounds*, who introduced himself as a fan, Bonham lifted the man by his lapels and screamed into his face: 'I've taken enough shit from you cunts in the press!'

On another occasion, also in LA, he went into a bar and ordered 20 Black Russians. Swigging down half of them he paused only to punch a female publicist who had been 'looking' at him, then returned to the bar to drink the other ten.

But perhaps the most daring Bonham escapade came in 1976, on the eve of the release of the *Presence* album. Bonham was at a Deep Purple concert on Long Island. During a particularly boring instrumental interlude he staggered on stage, watched by stunned roadies, and announced into a free microphone: 'I just want to tell you that we've got a new album coming out called *Presence* and it's fucking great. And as far as Tommy Bolin [Purple's guitarist] is concerned, he can't play for shit!'

The first sign that things were going to be terrible for the rest of Zeppelin's existence came in August 1975. The car carrying Robert Plant, his wife Maureen, who was driving, their children and Jimmy Page's daughter smashed into a tree in Rhodes after skidding on one of the island's treacherous roads. Maureen Plant suffered a fractured skull, her husband a broken ankle and elbow, and the children various broken limbs. Plant was told not to attempt to walk for at least six months.

It's been said that at this point Plant sobered up. He put part of the blame for the accident on Page's black magic dabbling. Plant denies this, but another associate of Page's, the American film director, Kenneth Anger, who was also a devotee of Crowley, saw fatal flaws in the guitarist's application of Crowley's dicta. For not only was Page, Anger reckoned, less than halfway to understanding the master's work, but his heroin habit was depleting his resources. Crowley had been a monster of a man and heroin had not weakened him physically, but Page was a mere will o' the wisp, becoming incoherent and brittle. That was the difference.

By now Page was not the only heroin dependant. Bonham was well past the stage of flirtation and most of the road crew were hooked as well.

Back at Boleskine House the vibes were getting out of hand. A caretaker

had killed himself, and his replacement had gone mad.

In July 1977 the greatest tragedy of all happened. Robert Plant's five-year-old son Karac died of a freak respiratory complaint. With this latest calamity for the Plant family to deal with the stories began to buzz: there was a curse on Zeppelin; Page had got it all horribly wrong; he had displeased his masters and now they were telling him about it.

Somehow the mystical musical glue that keeps bands together worked its spell on Zeppelin and they made one more album, the lacklustre *In Through The Out Door* in 1979. But then came the next tragedy and after this there could be no more.

It was 24 September 1980. John Bonham, on his way to a rehearsal at Page's Windsor house, stopped off at a pub for lunch. He washed down his sandwiches with sixteen vodkas. At the rehearsal which followed he continued to drink prolifically until he could no longer play. The rehearsal mutated into a party, with Bonham drinking vodka after vodka until he passed out. He was carried to a bedroom and left to sleep it off.

The next morning he would not respond to wake-up calls and when they turned him over they found that he was blue. The rock drummer extraordinaire, the man who played drum solos with his fists, had died at the age of 31.

Quite apart from any in-band fears of communal retribution for Page's irresponsibility in the past, it was obvious that Led Zeppelin was finished as a band. A statement to this effect appeared in the press in December of 1980.

And there it all stopped. Until the crazy summer day in 1985 when Bob Geldof persuaded the remaining three members back on to a stage with a guest drummer to help the Live Aid cause. The music they proceeded to play was an uncultured shambles, but it was nice to see them back doing it.

And then came 1988's surprise. At the 40th birthday celebrations for their former label, Atlantic Records, they reformed with John Bonham's 16-year-old son Jason on drums. Everyone assembled agreed that, if you closed your eyes, it was just like listening to the ruthless paramilitary clout of his old man.

# Prince

Nothing can be said with any degree of finality about Prince Rogers Nelson. His legend is as tricky as one of his guitar solos, his image as carefully applied as his make-up. Only two things are sure: he is small, and he is strange.

Prince has been recording since 1977, when his first album, *For You*, was the subject of mild amusement by virtue of its lyrical content. A credit to God on the sleeve seemed pretty out of place among some fairly blatant tributes to the sexual acts. However, paradoxically, sex and religion appear to have no problems co-existing on a Prince record. Between them they have constituted nearly all of his inspiration and a peek at his stage show will confirm that he draws equal pleasure from both.

His present superstar status – the only two non-political black Americans as famous as him are Mike Tyson and Michael Jackson – is not the transient affair that most rock stars enjoy. There seems no question of Prince ever becoming obsolete. There is probably no way he'll even be out of date. And one look at his prolific output since 1983, when the double album *1999* opened the commercial floodgates, suggests that he isn't even close to running out of ideas. What seems much more likely, if he *is* to fade from the limelight, is that internal traumas and massive self-doubts will be the causes. For, at the moment, Prince – quite simply – seems to believe that he is God.

It started to get heavy in 1984. The reason may have been the invisibility of Michael Jackson, for although the Jacko chart input was still spectacular, the album *Thriller*, from which all the singles were being culled, was by then two years old, and people were getting impatient for new product. They found a man called Prince, who had been releasing records of a highly sexual and exciting nature for several years, and who appeared to be

Prince

approaching some kind of creative watershed. They sat back and were prepared for disappointment. Most of them are still waiting for disappointment. Prince simply will not slow down.

The sexual content of his lyrics is phenomenally high, thanks to albums like *Dirty Mind* and *Controversy*, which between them dealt with a whole array of spicy subjects such as oral sex, incest and masturbation. When he was not singing about the peripherals he was singing about the original. 'Sex-related fantasy is all my mind can see,' he sang.

It was this attention to detail that won him the wrath of the 'Washington Wives' – the Parents' Music Resource Center, or PMRC – who found a wealth of pornographic imagery in his lyrics. Songs such as 'Darling Nikki' (specimen lyric: 'I met her in a hotel lobby/Masturbating with a magazine') and 'Let's Pretend We're Married' (easy to surmise) were singled out for the special rage of these custodians of taste, although what all these middle-aged women were listening to when Little Richard and Jerry Lee Lewis were singing remains anyone's guess. Prince's tendency to have a bed on stage with him just in case of emergencies must have peeved them even more.

And it was not just the Washington Wives who were after him. The Moral Majority had seen the regular 'thanks-to-God' sleeve notes and could not reconcile this apparent devotion with the lustful lyrical pyrotechnics.

Prince hysteria came in 1984 with the release of the *Purple Rain* film and soundtrack. It rivalled Jackson's *Thriller* as the best selling album ever in vinyl form, and secured the attention of tabloid newspapers everywhere in celluloid form. This new freaky 5 ft 2 in (157 cm) star was perceived to be a dynamic and resonant influx in a rather unexciting year. The press resolved to stick around. Unfortunately, Prince had decreed in 1982 that he would never give another interview again, as long as he lived, ever. It messed around with his heart rate or something. For want of fact, fiction became the necessity.

Britain at large got its first chance to see Prince in January, 1985, at the annual BPI awards. When he was announced he stood up in an outrageous purple get-up and walked behind his minder Chick Huntsberry – a human megalith – to the stage. The fact that the audience was made up of fellow performers, none of whom, one presumes, had any intention of attacking him, did not deter him from keeping them all at a very safe distance. Once on the stage he approached the microphone and mumbled something incoherent about God and traipsed off.

Holly Johnson of Frankie Goes To Hollywood made a joke at his expense at the same awards and the whole gathering seemed relieved to be able to vent their spleen in laughter at this strange young American. The next day Prince had made the papers. His behaviour was called 'extraordinary'.

Prince announced that he wouldn't ever be coming to Britain again because people had not shown him enough respect.

Prince has always been a loner, musically. While he is quite happy to sponsor groups with one of his songs he tends to record his own records himself, playing all the instruments and doing all the singing. He was probably the only major American artist not to appear on the star-studded USA For Africa single 'We Are The World'. Even Bob Dylan had been persuaded to cough a line or two but Prince was nowhere. Likewise, at the 1985 American Music Awards, he refused to join in on the 'We Are The World' sing-song, thereby getting up the backs of many who saw the Lionel Richie/Quincy Jones project as much more sacred than any one artist.

His prima donna antics were very soon the subject of much mirth. His twitchy face, sort of a cross between Jimi Hendrix and Charlie Chaplin, was ridiculed on puppet shows and unkind conjecture about his sexual proclivities was spread about.

When, in March 1985, he announced that he was retiring from live shows and going off 'to look for the ladder', a sizeable portion of the musical population believed this to be a good time for the straitjacket to be applied. What he meant, as became clear later in the year, was that he was going to look for 'The Ladder'. This was a lofty concept articulated in his much-maligned 'psychedelic' album, *Around The World In A Day*. He delivered the tapes of this record to Warner Bros accompanied by an entourage that Gloria Swanson in *Sunset Boulevard* would have been grateful to grace. He then sat on the floor surrounded by flowers while the WB boffins got to grips with the product. It all sounded very ominous – and would it sell?

The move towards *Sgt. Pepper*-type psychedelia confounded all those who had discovered him at the time of *Purple Rain* and expected something similar as a follow-up. But the move towards *Purple Rain* itself had disturbed all those who had stuck with Prince since the saucy postcard era of the late Seventies. It all pointed to one conclusion: clearly, Prince could not be second-guessed. At least the *Around The World* album was consistent in one factor: there was the legend 'all thanks 2 God' (Prince is the worst speller since Slade) on the sleeve.

This album had been credited to 'Prince And The Revolution'. The Revolution was not so much a group as a family of friends and girlfriends whom he could call on to play specialist parts. His chain of girlfriend/backing singers has included Vanity, Apollonia (with whom he starred in *Purple Rain*) and Sheena Easton, the chirpy Scots chanteuse who shot to fame thanks to Esther Rantzen's philanthropic TV show 'The Big Time'. She reputedly left him because he never spoke to her. Instead, he expected her to communicate with him by means of ESP.

Aficionados were less than overwhelmed with his next album, *Parade* (1986), although the single taken from it, 'Kiss', was hailed as a masterpiece. In March of that year two Princian bodyguards were sentenced to two years' probation, fined $500 and ordered to do 100 hours of community work for beating up some photographers who had tried to take pics of the puny maestro.

The singer's behaviour reached off-the-wall saturation level. He made a movie called *Under The Cherry Moon* which was universally reviled, some of the reviews actually descending to prolonged abuse. He started work on a new musical project which became the legendary lost album, or 'The Black Album'. This was first mentioned in the Warner Bros soon-come list in 1986, then mysteriously withdrawn. Bootleg tapes circulated, however, and it certainly sounded like a fine album. An explanation as to why it was held back eventually came from the man himself, in a surprisingly cogent and articulate statement sent to Warner Bros. Here is one paragrah:

'Spooky Electric must die. Die in the hearts of all who want love. Die in the hearts of men who want change. Die in the bodies of women who want babies that will grow up with a New Power Soul Love Life Lovesexy – the feeling u get when u fall in love, not with a girl or boy but with the heavens above. Lovesexy – endorphin. Camille figured out what 2 feel. Glam Slam Escape – the Sexuality Real.'

What would appear to be going on here is that Prince is having alter-ego problems. He has divided his psyche into two opposite trends. There is Spooky Electric, the lustful urchin in search of cool women and cheap thrills. And there is Camille, who only cares about the future of the world.

Having sorted that little problem out, Prince toured Britain to great acclaim in 1988. His album *Sign ☮ The Times* was deemed 'a bit more bloody like it' from all quarters and he was once again in the ascendant.

Still, the best stories come from the fizzy days. Of how he wrote to Miles Davis, the greatest living jazzman and a fan of Prince's, warning him that his popularity was on a noticeable downstroke and that, should he wish to reverse this trend, he really ought to come over and hang out with Prince.

Prince signed the letter 'God'.

# Groupies

The groupie scene was a phenomenon of the late Sixties and early Seventies, and various threatening social diseases have effectively put the mockers on groupiedom in the Eighties, much to the chagrin of some straggling leftover rock 'n' rollers who remember the good times.

It was at its height in the late Sixties havens of San Francisco, Los Angeles and New York. In 1969 the groupies knew they had arrived when the influential magazine *Rolling Stone* dedicated an entire issue to groupies, their philosophy, their quirks, their motivation and – in a few cases – their regrets.

What is/was a groupie? A groupie is a girl who hangs out with rock 'n' roll groups. Simple as that. Except that gradually the behaviour of certain of the groupie sorority got the more socially-minded ones a bad name, and groupies became a by-word for sex objects.

The whole question of following a rock musician to a hotel room and then enquiring about the possibilities of having sex with him and/or any of his friends and/or the road crew and/or anyone else who may be involved, however tenuously, with the rich and reckless world of rock 'n' roll seems like an amazingly ephemeral, not to say thankless, way to go about one's life. But there were those who had it down to a fine art. And for them the rewards were just as meaningful as, say, an auditorium full of screaming fans would be for the rock stars they pursued.

Not that a groupie existed as a mere sexual gift. There was the matter of entertainment, of company, of fun, of help around the house, of – well, what the hell – of love. As Jimmy Page of Led Zeppelin put it, 'The sex angle is important. But no more important than girls who are also good friends and make you feel like family.'

The appeal in actually *being* a groupie must have tormented parents of every teenage girl in the entire United States Of America at one time or another during the Sixties and Seventies. It basically seemed to come down to the irresistible temptation of four separate intoxicating agents, all dressed up in a vital cocktail. Number one, the sexual thrill, not to be underestimated. Number two, the drug thrill, which very often went hand in hand with number one. Number three, the thrill that the sex and drugs were being indulged in with a rock 'n' roll star. And number four, and most crucially, the cosmically inescapable thought that did not all this indulgence in sex and drugs on a regular basis with many and various rock 'n' roll stars make you a bit of a rock 'n' roll star too, by proxy?

The appeal in being around groupies was obvious and visceral. As Country Joe McDonald, a by no means negligible target for groupies in the late Sixties, put it, 'Groupies are beautiful. They come to hear you play, they throw flowers and underpants, they give you kisses and love, they come to bed with you. They're beautiful. We love groupies.'

This made it seem as though the groupies were charmingly naive little nymphettes who had, through a mixture of incorrect education and mind-expanding drugs, hit upon the notion that a woman's place is in a rock star's hotel room. Not so. Many of them were shrewd, streetwise and businesslike. Not for nothing was the groupie's successful conquest of a rock musician called a 'hit'.

Most groupies were very young, some of them extraordinarily so, and very few of them were genuinely undeniably beautiful. There was a tendency among groupies to go mad with make up to try to adopt a strong, personal, individual look. Many of them lined their eyes with charcoal. Some went for the flowers and raindrops effect. There was real rivalry.

There was also inter-city rivalry. It was rock lore that New York groupies were the best-looking, San Francisco ones the most friendly and amenable to long-standing, meaningful relationships. And Los Angeles girls would do anything.

It was somehow appropriate that the Los Angeles groupie scene was sewn up by Frank Zappa, the musician who would do anything.

Zappa's patronage of the groupies was not just for obvious reasons. He really saw artistic merit in their efforts. The first thing he did was to gather together tapes of conversations with Los Angeles groupies, then their diaries, letters etc., and write a book called The Groupie Papers (unpublished). Then he sponsored the notorious Plastercasters Of Chicago.

These two were a real reflection on how liberal things had gotten by 1968. Cynthia (early 20s) and Diane (late teens) Plastercaster (unlikely – but then very few groupies had surnames) were in the habit of approaching famous rock stars of the day and asking them if they would be interested in having their genitals cast in plaster of Paris for posterity's sake. More often than not they were greeted with warm acceptance.

They took their work seriously, even to the point of getting business cards printed and carrying attaché cases, and they were nothing if not ambitious. 'I'd love to get the President,' said one of the duo once.

Zappa for his part was extremely coy. No, he had not been cast himself (not his style) but he would not hear a word against the girls. 'I want to make one thing clear in front [!]. The girls don't think this is the least bit creepy, and neither do I.'

However, Zappa kept his best stroke for the GTO's. This stood for Girls Together Outrageously (although some folks, seeing a possible lesbian scoop suggested it was Girls Together Only) who were a six-piece singing group. Zappa affiliated them to his more-freaks-please record labels

Straight/Bizarre and they were pretty awful. The Mothers Of Invention, who really could play, showed much contempt for this project of Zappa's. But Zappa was adamant. He'd heard of how two of them liked to dance around in diapers, and that was good enough for him.

No offence to Mr Zappa, but he was not even in the top ten of desirable hits. Those places were resolved almost exclusively for visiting English musicians of the calibre of Jimmy Page and Jeff Beck, and only Jimi Hendrix could claim to be the top US representative. That figured. The guitarist 'only remembered a city for its chicks'.

But the groupies did not have it all their own way. Jeff Beck and Eric Clapton particularly were unimpressed by the groupie scenario.

'These groupies, you know, they've never got anything to say for themselves. I've seen them all and it's depressing. Groupies use groups, not the reverse. It's all for their own egos' (Jeff Beck). 'It wasn't your body or your face they wanted to make love to, but your name' (Eric Clapton).

# Sex Changes and Missing Limbs

The wonderful world of rock 'n' roll, which is now nearing the dubious respectability produced by length of service – over 30 years – has been generally peopled by personalities whose physical perfection made them fully paid up members of the potential idol class, with the notable exception of punks, many of whom seemed to feel that musical ability and normal appearance were a positive handicap to their ambitions.

Spare a thought, then, for those unfortunate individuals who had no great desire for punk stardom, yet were the unfortunate victims of fate in losing a limb, but still managed to achieve some kind of fame. There are certainly more of these particularly courageous people than we shall discuss, but probably the three most celebrated members of this exclusive club are Sandy Nelson, Victor Maltoa (aka Moulty of The Barbarians) and Rick Allen, each of whom was short of a hand or a leg.

Nelson was a drummer who lost part of his left leg in a car accident. He had already made a name for himself before the crash with international Top 10 hit 'Teen Beat' in 1959. 'Let There Be Drums', which also reached the Top 10 on both sides of the Atlantic was actually recorded shortly after he lost his foot, but seemed to cause him little inconvenience, and he went on to release two more hits, 'Drums Are My Beat' and 'Drummin' Up A Storm' in 1962, before making his final chart appearance with the updated version of his first hit, 'Teen Beat '65', which was apparently released in 1964 (!). It would probably be true to say that the critical loss of one quarter of a drummer's armoury was less responsible for Nelson's fall from grace than the fact that each of his hits featured drums as lead instrument. Such a gimmick possesses a certain contagious quality, some might say, and this cannot be denied, yet many might say that to reach the chart five times in six years with records which predominantly consist of drumming made Nelson an extremely fortunate person. This does not in any way compensate for the loss of his foot, of course.

Next comes Moulty, another drummer. The Barbarians, who came from Boston, Massachusetts, would probably have been a punk band had the genre been invented and the word coined to apply to rock as early as the mid-Sixties, when they were briefly famous. Maltoa (he probably got his nickname from his real surname being mis-pronounced) had a metal hook instead of his left hand. It may be peculiarly British to feel that drawing attention to such a handicap is not quite the correct thing to do, and as Moulty was an American, perhaps one can excuse the group's final US Top 40 hit, which is not only sung by but also titled 'Moulty'. It's jolly touching, too. Moulty tells us all about how he has to constantly fight his affliction, accompanied by a keening harmonica. He goes on to explain that what keeps him going is his love of music, success at which is an ultimate achievement. The record closes with Moulty advertising for a girlfriend, who will not love him out of sympathy but out of real affection. Whether he found such a lady or not is not recorded in books (or on vinyl, as far as can be ascertained), but despite his and The Barbarians' appearance in the cult rock movie, *The TAMI Show*, the group and Moulty have yet to score a hit to follow 'Moulty', although it is remembered as something of a milestone in the musical annals of its era.

Rick Allen wasn't so lucky, although his story parallels that of Sandy Nelson rather than Moulty. The drummer with immensely successful Sheffield hard rockers Def Leppard, whose third album, *Pyromania*, sold several million copies, Allen had invested in a sports car with part of his substantial earnings, and as the group basked in huge popularity, took a girlfriend for a spin one evening. The car crashed and Allen lost an arm, which delayed the recording of a new album, as his colleagues were decent enough to let him recover. When a new album did emerge in 1987, it equalled the sales of *Pyromania* in considerably less time. *Hysteria*, as it's called, must be regarded as an even bigger hit than its predecessor, which makes Allen the most successful of this percussionistic triumvirate.

It is almost certain that the mental anguish of losing a limb is quite different from the anguish which must exist in those who submit to sex change operations. Once again, a trio of unfortunates may not be the total of those in music who have felt that nature made a mistake, but just as each of the three without a limb were drummers, each of this sex change triad were once male but are now female. Wally Stott was an acclaimed musician, an orchestra leader whose work can be heard and appreciated on several early Dusty Springfield hits. At a certain point, Stott became Angela Morley, who continued to work as an orchestrator, one of her more successful projects being the incidental musical score for the cartoon rabbit film, *Watership Down*. The information that her children still call Ms Morley 'dad' may be apocryphal.

Wally Stott/Angela Morley was not an outrageous figure, and the same is true, as far as can be discovered from this side of the Atlantic, of Walter/Wendy Carlos, whose imaginative album, *Switched On Bach*, which featured compositions by Johann Sebastian of that ilk played on synthesizer, was released in 1969 and sold over a million copies. The 1970s, a decade which brought Carlos further acclaim in the shape of the soundtrack to Kubrick's celebrated cult movie, *A Clockwork Orange*, was also the period during which Walter became Wendy. As in the case of Stott/Morley, the operation had little effect on Walter/Wendy's ability, and she contributed to the soundtrack of another of Stanley Kubrick's celebrated feature films, *The Shining*.

To suggest that Wayne/Jayne County was not outrageous is to sell this extremely famous transsexual punk short. Wayne was a transvestite actor who played the role of Florence Nightingale in a New York production, *World – Birth Of A Nation*. He arrived in Britain as a member of the cast of an Andy Warhol play titled *Pork*, and impressed David Bowie sufficiently for the latter to sign County to his production company. On his return to New York, County led a band called Queen Elizabeth, an original punk group who were contemporaries of the New York Dolls (some of whom looked like females although they were all certainly male). Wayne's stage attire apparently consisted of a blonde wig, fishnet stockings, heaps of make up and a dress. The Bowie connection produced little, so County continued on his own, forming a new group called the Electric Chairs, whose most celebrated song, 'If You Don't Want To Fuck Me, Fuck Off', was included on an EP with the remarkably accurate title 'Blatantly Offensive'. Another song on the EP, 'Toilet Love', includes the lyrical line 'I love it when you smell my dirty socks', among other dubious verses. Thereafter, Wayne became Jayne, but where Stott/Morley and Carlos appeared not to have lost much of their inspiration after their operations, County fairly quickly fell into obscurity. Many may feel such a fate particularly well-deserved.

# ...DRUGS and...

Mick Jagger and Marianne Faithfull

# The Rolling Stones

With the cool detached precision of a dedicated user-abuser Keith Richards dips the tiny spoon in the bag and brings it up to his nose. His risky-gypsy features contort and, one sniff later, the norm is resumed. He passes the bag across to the journalist.

The journalist accepts, mute, thrilled to be co-opted on to the board. He fumbles at first and hopes to God the great man hasn't noticed his lack of expertise. Seconds later he is in the lap of the Gods, artistically licensed, jack-plugged, coked to the eyeballs. He has taken cocaine with Keith Richards.

A few minutes later the process is repeated. And again, a few minutes after that. Eventually the journalist is running on a dangerously combustible level, a mass of speeding heart, mind and limbs. His cheeks – if only he could feel them – are so hollow they are almost concave.

Richards lets him get on with it for an hour or so. Then he sidles across with some of his notoriously Grade A heroin (streets are for singing about, not for scoring on) and the man from the music press passes out in a blank, luxurious swoon on the plush Chelsea carpet.

Keith Richards' long-lived relationship with drugs has been well documented. His lifestyle would have destroyed lesser mortals years ago. But the reason Richards continues, in his own cavalier way, to exist is because he is a connoisseur. Denying that he has a problem with drugs, 'only a problem with cops', he has been the subject of spectacular, salacious rumours: he has his blood changed twice a year; he never sleeps; he can't remember the Seventies, any of it.

And following the rumours, in quick succession, the predictions: he'll be dead in a year; he'll be dead in an hour; he'll drop dead on a stage, in the middle of one of his legendary bastardised Chuck Berry solos. And the bandit grin on what remains of his middle-aged face will vanish and one famous quote will hang in the air:

'If they take the fun out of this life, I'll *leave*.'

It was an ambition of pure intent. The Rolling Stones would be a faithful and exciting testimonial to the electric blues, fashioned by their original leader Brian Jones in the musical styles of Elmore James, Muddy Waters and Chuck Berry.

Harangued by the trad jazz set and ignored by most of their own generation on their inception in 1962, they built up a strong following in R&B clubs and were approached by a young, flashy fix-it merchant by the name of Andrew Oldham who was armed with something of a reputation (having done publicity for Brian Epstein's NEMS company), an eye for a scoop, a literary style purloined from Anthony Burgess's *A Clockwork Orange*, and a Decca recording contract. Under his guidance The Stones had their first hit in 1963.

The Stones' line-up divided neatly into three factions. The first was the Mick Jagger–Keith Richards axis. Cajoled by Oldham into writing original material for their first album, they began spending more and more time together, re-establishing the friendship they had had as small boys in Dartford, Kent.

The second, and most clearly defined, was the rhythm section of Bill Wyman and Charlie Watts. With no say in the proceedings and no superstar aspirations, they lurked at the back of the stage, hunched over their respective instruments.

This left on his own the most complex member of the group – Brian Jones. Jones had founded the band in his own likeness – dedicated, talented, sneering, mischievous, artistic, raffish and almost dangerously heterosexual. Banished from the streets of his home-town, Cheltenham, Gloucestershire, for impregnating two girls by the age of 16, he lived for just three things: clothes, R&B and stardom. Visually the most striking of the band, he was also the most prodigiously talented, being able to play practically any instrument in the band. But he had many personality problems beneath the surface.

'Brian was brought up in the worst possible way,' Keith Richards has said. 'He had a very good education, was very clever at school, but somewhere along the line he decided he was going to be a full-time professional rebel, and it didn't really suit him. So that when he wanted to be obnoxious, he had to really make an effort, and having made the effort, he would be really obnoxious. I don't want to be too hard on Brian. He was a very difficult person.'

Increasingly erratic, struck down on occasions by chronic asthma attacks and just generally a liability, Brian began – ever so subtly – to be phased out. Interviews were handled by Mick and Keith. Brian was never considered as a possible songwriter. Pills and drink conspired to hospitalize him. As early as 1965 his doctor told him he would be dead in a year if he didn't stop drinking.

In September of that year Brian met Anita Pallenberg, a woman who would have an incalculable influence on the lives of at least three of The Stones over the course of the next ten years. A major European model-turned-actress, she was attracted first to Brian because of all The Stones he was the only one who bothered to speak to her. He even spoke a little German, her native language. Now with three illegitimate sons (the last two of which in an act of gratuitous mischief he had christened by the same name, although he preferred to refer to the third by the nickname 'Broad Bean Head'), Brian invited Anita to live with him in London. She became his lover, his spiritual adviser and even, in a certain light, his exact double – a fact which did not escape seasoned Brian-watchers. She persuaded him to be photographed wearing an SS uniform, stamping on a doll with his jack-boots. The photo caused a furore in the British press.

Earlier that year The Rolling Stones had experienced the first in what would prove to be a long line of court visits. It transpired that on an evening in March a chauffeur-driven Daimler had stopped at a service station in East London and out of it had stepped a 'shaggy-haired monster'. The monster was Bill Wyman and his mission was the immediate location of a urinal. Informed that it was out of order he summoned reinforcements from the Daimler and eight or nine people jumped out. Mick Jagger pushed the garage-owner out of the way with the words, 'we piss anywhere man', and he, Brian Jones and Wyman proceeded to empty their bladders in a line, against the wall of the forecourt. They were found guilty of 'insulting behaviour' and fined £3 each.

The predictably outraged headlines in the tabloid press were easily laughed away but the sheer weight of press opinion directed against them should have told The Stones what to expect. One day in early 1967, nauseated by countless rumours of sordid drug frenzies and bacchanalian orgies to which none of them had been invited, the combined forces of journalistic and detective talent on the News Of The World decided that it was about time something was done about The Rolling Stones.

The most obvious solution was to catch them in the drug-taking act. It was well known that they indulged with chilling frequency in marijuana, and it was strongly believed that pills were involved too somewhere along the line. There was a rumour about a new drug of awesome hallucinogenic power called LSD which a very cosmic British group had been caught taking.

Therefore, further incensed by the refusal of The Rolling Stones to observe a quaint British custom – that performers on Sunday Night At The London Palladium shall congregate at the end of the programme on a revolving stage and wave cheerily to the audience – the News Of The World went out to get itself a story.

It got it all wrong.

It started promisingly enough. Mick Jagger came into the club where the reporters were waiting, consented to be interviewed and pleaded guilty to all the charges. Yes, he took marijuana, it was great. Yes, he took acid, that was even better.

In gleeful capital letters it was spelled out. The News Of The World had caught Jagger bang to rights. Except that in its hurry to get the story the newspaper had forgotten to check the names with the faces. It was not Mick Jagger they had been talking to but Brian Jones, whose insouciance was legendary.

It is quite likely that the story would have stopped right there, in a garbled report of hilariously righteous prose and mangled facts, had not Mick Jagger been booked to appear on the Eamonn Andrews Show on the Sunday the story broke.

Questioned about the matter he

announced that it was all a lie and that a libel writ against the newspaper would be issued. When they heard this, the *News Of The World* set out to fix The Stones once and for all.

It has never been established where the tip-off came from. The facts are that at Keith Richards' country house in Sussex a group of 11 people including Richards himself, Mick Jagger along with his girlfriend, Marianne Faithfull, George Harrison and his wife, and a few close friends and hangers-on assembled for a weekend party. Jagger, who despite his 'confession' to the *News Of The World* had not yet tried LSD, was intrigued by reports from close friends, and one of their number, David Schneidermann (the self-titled 'Acid King'), had come equipped with a leather attaché case full of it.

Sunday passed in quiet relaxation, tripping on acid and touring the nearby countryside. Harrison and his wife left and the guests returned to watch TV.

A knock came at the door.

When the police busted Richards' house they found all but one – Richards' servant – lying in a giggling zoo of long hair and pillows: Richards was laughing, asking them to be careful not to ruin the patterns on the carpet; Marianne Faithfull was dressed in nothing but a fur rug; the Acid King's case of LSD was on the floor in full view; Robert Fraser, an art dealer and friend of Richards', was a heroin addict and had plenty of it in his pocket as well as some uppers and some hashish.

It looked bad for most of them but Jagger, having no drugs in his possession, was sure he had no cause for alarm. It would later come out in court that Marianne Faithfull had treated the raid as a huge joke, flashing to the policemen and making remarks about 'dykes' when a policewoman tried to search beneath the rug she was wearing. She had earlier deposited four amphetamine uppers in a green velvet jacket of Jagger's, and forgotten about them. Jagger, faced with the evidence, made the most gallant gesture of his life by admitting that they were his, but added that he had been prescribed them. He even named the doctor.

The Stones were not believed. Richards was sentenced to one year's imprisonment for allowing marijuana to be smoked on his premises. Fraser got six months for possessing heroin and amphetamines. Jagger, who burst into tears when his sentence was announced, received three months.

Of course there was more to the court case than a list of drugs followed by a verdict. Maximum mileage was obtained from Faithfull's near-naked condition, plus the thought-provoking fact that she was 'apparently enjoying the situation' and 'in merry mood'. Rumours of astonishing bestiality and decadence have plagued The Stones since but none has been so fascinating and hard to dispel as the rumour that swept Britain during that court case – that when the police raided the house Mick Jagger was on his knees, his enormous Michelin Man lips licking a Mars Bar embedded in Marianne Faithfull's vagina.

Outrage greeted the sentences. William Rees-Mogg, then editor of *The Times*, risked prosecution by commenting on a *sub judice* case. In his editorial, which he entitled, 'Who Breaks a Butterfly on a Wheel?', a quotation from William Blake, he condemned the sentences and more pertinently the atmosphere of smug, narrow-minded righteousness with which they had been arrived at.

Meanwhile the Acid King had disappeared off the face of the earth. It is now widely believed that he was employed to set up The Stones, since he escaped prosecution – ludicrously, since he was laden with LSD – although the *News Of The World* categorically denied having hired him.

On appeal the jail sentences were quashed although Jagger's conviction stood. His sentence was commuted to one year's conditional discharge. Later that day, heavily sedated and barely comprehensible, he faced the World In Action TV cameras in a debate chaired by Rees-Mogg in which he denied himself to be anything other than a musician.

Brian Jones had intended joining the party that weekend. However, in a rare burst of musical activity, he had been working on a soundtrack for a new film which would star Anita Pallenberg. He escaped the raid by hours. And walked straight into another one.

It was astonishing in a way that it took so long for the Brian Jones debut

bust to happen; he was notoriously lax in habit and behaviour, decadent in public as well as private, living in a frantic netherworld of clubs, alcohol and narcotics. Tony Sanchez, 'Spanish Tony', his nasal attaché, was employed exclusively as his minder. 'The only reality Brian wanted was oblivion,' he says.

Jones was busted at his London flat and charged with possession of cocaine, methedrine and cannabis resin. On bail, he began to see a psychiatrist. He was sentenced to concurrent prison terms of nine months and three months.

On appeal, and on the recommendation of the psychiatrist, this was commuted to a £1,000 fine and he was put on probation for three years. The last of those three years would prove to be unnecessary.

Following a second bust in May 1968, Brian plunged into a state of almost psychotic despair. Convinced that the other Stones were plotting to replace him (if he was imprisoned this time he would miss the next tour and there were rumours that Eric Clapton was about to disband his group Cream), he succeeded in kicking all his drug dependencies but hit the bottle with a vengeance. His weight shot up, his blond hair looked thick and unwashed and his face became bloated. In a display of extreme – reporters at the time said unprecedented – leniency he was fined £50 and told not to be so naughty again.

Later that year he bought Cotchford

Farm in Sussex. It was a child's idyll, the house where little Christopher Robin had frolicked as a boy while A. A. Milne wrote about him and his funny friends Eeyore and Winnie the Pooh. These days the house boasted a large swimming pool.

Exasperating everyone with his now totally unreliable personality (he was no longer playing on Stones records, aiming his acoustic guitar at a microphone that, had he looked closer, he would have seen was not plugged in), Brian was asked to leave. In May 1969 he agreed not to be a Rolling Stone any longer. In the early hours of 3 July he went for a swim in his pool and remained in the water until his lifeless body was discovered and dragged out. He was 26.

Three days later Mick Jagger walked on to a stage in Hyde Park in what looked like an obscene transvestite outfit. He instructed the quarter of a million expectant fans to 'cool it' for a minute and proceeded to quote Shelley in a poetic tribute to the man who had founded The Rolling Stones, given them their name, direction and early image, and died in a swimming pool purchased with their riches.

Hundreds of white butterflies were released into the air; white, virginal and beautiful, they were to be the ultimate tribute. Most of them had died, however, suffocated in their boxes.

That winter The Stones toured America in what would prove to be the epitome of the rock'n'roll nightmare.

They antagonized and alienated journalists and fans alike with their exorbitant ticket prices and irritating tendency not to play until they had exhausted the contents of the drugs cabinet. And eventually, at Altamont, the spirit of freedom and optimism of the late Sixties perished for all time to the tune of one of their songs.

Altamont, those with a sense of irony have observed, was supposed to be a gift. A way of saying thank you – and, it is just conceivable, sorry – to the kids of America who had followed the hectic events of the blockbusting tour. At the Altamont Raceway, a stock-car racing track in California, The Stones, pressurized by complaints of excess and contempt for their audience, decided to give a free festival. The Grateful Dead, who knew the area and were famous for their free shows, advised them that the local Hell's Angels would make admirable security guards, putting the sheen of good vibes and self-control on the whole show.

This seemed fair enough. The Stones hated having the police at their gigs and anyway the London Hell's Angels had policed Hyde Park in subtle and laudable fashion earlier in the year. Jagger and Richards probably admired the image of the Angels too: irrepressible rogues, life's true wanderers, cinematic rebels, locked in a fraternity of women, drugs and booze.

It had been a traumatic year. Woodstock's example of goodwill and communal nudity had been tarnished by violence at other copycat festivals. Drugs had got out of hand; political groups were muscling in; Manson was slicing people up in the name of rock 'n' roll; and songs about revolution were being taken just a little too literally for their authors' liking.

Jagger, who wrote about war, Satan and the Boston Strangler, was bringing a noticeable edge of sinister evil to his performances. Richards was increasingly fuelled on heroin. The whole thing was getting a little scary. Altamont, it was hoped, would cool everybody down.

The toll of four deaths seems, in retrospect, incredible. The official film of the event, *Gimme Shelter*, shot under conditions of extreme danger by the Maysles brothers, tells a dark, nasty tale: at first menace and bad karma as people freak out on site and Jagger is attacked by a kid; then sporadic violence as Hell's Angels lose their tempers at the freaks. Members of Jefferson Airplane are threatened and beaten up by the very people they believed should be running the country.

The Stones come on stage about eight hours later than scheduled. Word has it that Jagger thinks he will look more impressive in the dark. Angels are by now laying into anyone who looks at them the wrong way. Pool cues fly, kids exit bleeding and Jagger steps up to address his party guests. 'Brothers and sisters,' he exhorts them in his weird Home-Counties-meets-Truman-Capote twang, 'just cool out now . . .' His voice sounds flat,

powerless and not a little concerned. The stage is only a few feet high and there are Angels milling around, looking at him with the abattoir eyes of drugged, drunken animals.

The set breaks down again and again. 'Cats' are urged to 'cool it' or the band will 'split'. The argot impresses no-one. People are terrified, seriously afraid for their lives. The hundreds of thousands of dazed hippy kids are seeing the beautiful vision explode in hues of black and red at the hands of a few greasy Hell's Angels who have been given $500 worth of free beer on condition that they do not fling the empty cans at the stage.

The murder of Meredith Hunter happens, not as was widely believed at the time, during 'Sympathy For The Devil', although a murder nearly did take place during that song ('we always have something very funny happen when we play that song'). It is while new guitarist Mick Taylor is negotiating the chords of 'Under My Thumb' that the tall black boy in the gaudy green suit makes a desperate leap for safety. Hounded by Angels for being black and grinning a lot, as well as being in the company of a white girl, he flashes a gun. He is stabbed once, twice, then disappears in a melée of skulls and crossbones. Attempts to revive him prove fruitless when the blood begins to seep through the green jacket. The Stones play on.

The morning after, it was generally felt that the day had been something of a success. Although four had died (apart from the murder of Meredith

Hunter there had been three accidental deaths) there had been an equal number of births, lots of people had been privileged to hear some great music (it is reckoned that The Rolling Stones played one of their finest gigs at Altamont) and after all nobody had had to pay to get in.

Then the true reports started filtering in. Nobody had been born at Altamont. It had been a day of destruction and fear. A few Hell's Angels' motorbikes had been knocked over and the stoned, naked freaks had paid the penalty.

The Rolling Stones were condemned in the press for their gross conceit and superstar hubris and especially for their lack of contrition.

*Rolling Stone* magazine, which had taken its name from the group, was scathing in its criticism, with Jagger being singled out, scorned for his helplessness in the face of real demons.

Whereas The Beatles' innocence had manifested itself merely in disastrous business ventures and Lennon-inspired follies, The Stones, getting meaner and meaner, riding on the fiery wings of 'Sympathy For The Devil', 'Midnight Rambler' and 'Street Fighting Man', were challenging the skulls and the bones to react. And in the warm, sticky twilight the words of the song that defined evil in 1969, as sung by a 26-year-old from Kent, echoed round the Altamont Raceway: 'I'll stick my knife right down your throat, baby. And it *hurts*.'

With Brian Jones's 'death by misadventure' verdict had come the inevitable raised eyebrows. He went for a swim at midnight? And nobody saw him drown? Wasn't he supposed to be a first-rate swimmer?

Suicide had been ruled out. Everyone who saw him during his last few days alive remarked on how happy he had seemed, how he had all sorts of plans for forming a new blues band dedicated to his new Mississippi visions.

In 1983 the *News Of The World*'s magazine printed the revelations of a close friend of Jones who reportedly had proof that the guitarist had been murdered by drug-dealers whom he had double-crossed several years previously. The story, frustratingly enough, was written in time-honoured what-if format.

With Mick Taylor on guitar The Stones hit the Seventies in cavalier fashion. They were now writing their finest rock'n'roll, songs of thrilling rhythmic power like 'Brown Sugar', 'Bitch' and 'Loving Cup'. Their 1972 double-album *Exile On Main Street* is arguably the greatest rock album of all time.

However, the Richards–Jagger songwriting duo were becoming more and more estranged. Jagger, whose former girlfriend Marianne Faithfull had left him after a failed suicide attempt in Australia, was now married to Bianca Perez Mora Macías, a Nicaraguan gossip-columnist's dream whose physiognomy was uncannily similar to his own.

Richards, who had rescued Anita

Pallenberg from the fists of Brian Jones one night in Morocco, was holed up in a French mansion, hooked on heroin, becoming increasingly scornful of Jagger's jet set existence.

As it turned out, the Seventies would not be over-kind to any of them. Jagger's marriage collapsed in acrimony and his bank account came dangerously close to collapsing in alimony. In the event, Bianca got $1 million, having claimed twelve and a half. Jagger took up with model Jerry Hall and resumed his life of highly-mannered controversy, always cautious not to go too far.

His ex from the Sixties was having a bad time. Marianne Faithfull was as deep in the heroin morass as it is possible to get – scoring on the street, living rough, frequently waking up in a cell. Somehow she pulled herself out by the roots and forged a critically-acclaimed solo career as a cracked-voiced singer of painfully vulnerable laments.

Mick Taylor left in 1974. He hadn't even smoked before meeting The Stones. He was now a heroin addict. When John Phillips of The Mamas And The Papas visited him in 1976 he found him still battling the drug:

'I got his address from a friend, went over to Taylor's place, and knocked. He peeked through a hole in the door. We had met before but he didn't recognize me. I told him what I wanted but he snapped, "I haven't played a guitar in two years", and shut the peephole.'

The nightmare of Keith Richards

and Anita Pallenberg was gathering speed. Informed that he would not be allowed into the United States to participate in The Stones' tour of 1975 if his blood showed any trace of heroin, he entered a Swiss clinic. The rumours at the time were disarmingly blunt – Keith Richards was having his blood changed. His friend and dealer, 'Spanish' Tony Sanchez, recounts that Richards was delighted at this new state of affairs.

'It doesn't matter if I get hooked again now,' he is reputed to have said. 'I can give it up any time I like without any bother.'

Richards has subsequently scoffed at the blood-change stories. The truth, he maintains, is slightly less glamorous: he underwent excruciating cold turkey withdrawal treatment.

Whatever happened, he did get hooked again, and in February 1977 it seemed to be all over. Stopped at customs at Toronto airport, Anita was found in possession of hashish. Three days later the hotel room she shared with Richards was raided. As well as cocaine they found an ounce of pure heroin. This was enough to put him away for life.

It seemed pretty clear that The Rolling Stones were finished. Taylor had been replaced by the less acclaimed guitarist, Ron Wood, Wyman was muttering about leaving and their lead guitarist and backbone was about to be convicted on a charge of trafficking smack. 'Could This Be The Last Time?' asked one newspaper.

Twenty months later, Richards was released on condition he play a charity concert for the blind. The Canadian government, stunned by photos of the Prime Minister's wife, Margaret Trudeau, in the company of The Rolling Stones, and appalled by the fact that – yet again – a Rolling Stone was going to get away with it, appealed. Richards walked away cackling.

And Keith is clean today. Remorseless, flippant, even proud of his past, he plays on, crafting his inimitable five-string chords that no chart can accommodate, siring indirectly a whole legion of lookalikes, think-alikes and act-alikes. Totally underestimating the famous Richards constitution, however, they shoot up, fall down, burn out.

A blank generation of minor league rock musicians has sprung up in his wake, and the master looks like outliving them all.

He split from Anita Pallenberg, said to be a witch, weaving strange, malignant spells over all who crossed her. None of that seems to matter now. Bloated and beaten, she met the courts yet again in 1980 when a teenage boy shot himself at her house.

Her former lover has yet to die on stage. It probably won't happen – falling asleep during 'Fool To Cry' was the closest he's ever come – just as the much-vaunted Stones reunion tour probably won't happen. One day a quiet breath will fade to nothing and the tributes will start to flow for the rock'n'roll genius who left friends, lovers and enemies strewn along the bloody roads in his tireless odyssey for the good time to end them all.

# Janis Joplin

'I wanted to smoke dope, take dope, lick dope, suck dope, fuck dope, anything I could lay my hands on I wanted to do it . . . Hey, man, what is it? I'll try it. How do you do it? Do you suck it? No? You swallow it? I'll swallow it.' – Janis Joplin, 1970, a few months before her death.

Janis Joplin had the blues, and didn't she let the world know about it. If pain had a singing voice, it would sound a lot like the Joplin howl. Straight from the gut she sang, via her tortured soul and her broken heart. Even a line like, 'Oh Lord won't you buy me a Mercedes Benz' scorched in tones of raw hurt, symbolic of all the fine things in life Janis could not have – simple things like a pretty face, a loving husband, and maybe a couple of kids to make tomorrow something to look forward to.

In the 27 years of her life, tragically curtailed when she became yet another victim of heroin, she proved beyond any doubt that Sophie Tucker was in no way the *last* of the red hot mammas.

She came out of Port Arthur, Texas – an All-American, small, backward, fiercely proud, intermittently violent, thoroughly racist town of about 60,000 inhabitants, none of them like Joplin.

She shocked and delighted her parents with her sharp intelligence and precocious painting ability. She could read before she started school. Indeed, even in her bleakest hours of how-can-they-love-me self-doubt, even after the unqualified triumphs and unmitigated disasters, there was never a book very far away. It was an unfair myth that Janis Joplin was rescued from a life of mundane manual work by rock 'n' roll.

As she grew up, her fate was gradually sealed. Completely lacking the demure, cleavage-clenching prettiness of your average Southern belle (and possessing a terrible complexion), she became the focus for horrible abuse at her school. That, and a tendency to hang out with the boys, would shape her life. It would be a major heartbreak for her that men were perfectly content, willing even, to be seduced from the safe distance of a stage when she sang, but, once the show was over, she went home alone while they retreated into the arms of girls designed with more conventional ideas of beauty in mind.

Displaying a serious alcohol problem as early as the age of 17, she was admitted to the local hospital and subsequently saw a psychiatrist. It was clear that flight was necessary.

So off to Los Angeles she went, then to Venice Beach, and on her return to Port Arthur it was noticed by everyone that Janis was now a fully-fledged wildcat, combining a manic, head-on, hard drinking charm with a Californian-inspired beatnik lifestyle.

Her drinking habits changed. Out went the beer, in came the hard stuff. Crossing the Sabine River into the much funkier state of Louisiana she and her male friends would embark on trawls of sleazy bars, risking the madness and violence, scoring free drinks off the regulars.

In 1962 Janis entered the University of Texas. She immediately took up with a like-minded ghetto crowd, one of whose main passions was folk music. Janis was singing now. Her voice underwent several changes until she found her style (a whining bluegrass yodel was attempted but didn't sound right), and eventually her whisky voice slid into a bluesy Bessie Smith groove for the barking, pleading phrases that would become her trademark.

As ever, an undercurrent of depression was starting to taint the good times. In a display of slightly cruel humour the students of the university nominated her as the 'Ugliest Man on Campus'. Crushed by her irredeemable unpopularity, she upped and left, for San Francisco. It would be a long time before she returned.

In San Francisco her boozing habits got more and more extraordinary. Sipping almost constantly from a Bourbon bottle, she was also not averse to hanging out on street corners, shooting the breeze with chronic winos. She recognized fellow refugees when she saw them.

Janis Joplin

Another characteristic of San
Francisco in the early Sixties was the
ubiquity of speed. Janis dived in,
eager to embrace the drug of the
street, and it is quite likely that she
tried heroin too. She moved to New
York in 1964 and spent the summer
shooting speed. Returning to San
Francisco she began to deal to
finance her own addiction, becoming
increasingly strung out. Finally, in May
1965, she went to a San Francisco
hospital and declared herself to be
insane. Suspicious of her ragged
appearance, they turned her away.
Now, living with a shady character
whose habit matched her own, her
down-ride gathered pace. Aware that
this ride had only one way out, Janis
managed to pull herself together
before it was too late.

She returned to Port Arthur to a life
of long-sleeved dresses, parental
chats and tense, unfamiliar conformity.
There was a desperate attempt to
wean herself off speed. She managed
it thanks to a scrupulous routine of
college and family occasions, and also
a firm belief that she was to be
married to the slumped figure that had
shared her San Francisco nightmare.
That particular illusion was well and
truly shattered when the hapless
wretch arrived at the Joplin house and
announced that he was 'splitting'.

The rejection was taken seriously.
All that kept her from heading back to
oblivion was the belief that somewhere
deep down in her soul was a sweet
homely little housewife just waiting to
be given the chance.

In her feast of anxieties she began
to consider that relations with women
might be slightly less painful. An
ardent desire to get close to someone
– anyone – added to a genuine sense
of gratitude when somebody made
even a tentative sexual gambit in her
direction, meant that lesbian/straight
differentials went by the board, fogged
by her all-consuming need for the
human touch. To the outside world it
looked repulsive, but Janis Joplin
cared little for public opinion; there
was never any question of a
prospective partner being asked to fill
out an application form.

The ephemeral blasts which
constituted her sexual encounters
were in their own squalid way nothing
more sinister than compressed love
affairs – only casual, trivial and
meaningless when she awoke the
following morning, feeling nothing.

But at least she was singing again.
Eschewing the saccharine tones of
Joan Baez, which is certainly what the
Port Arthur audience expected from a
'chick' singer, she hit the blue notes
with a passion. Some success came
her way, however, and in time a call
came from San Francisco – there was
a band up there who needed exactly a
chick of her nature, could she drop
everything . . . ?

The band was Big Brother And The
Holding Company, a fairly rudimentary
but deafeningly loud blues outfit
whose unerring ability to hit four
different wrong beats instead of one
good one was made irrelevant by the
fact that they were all out of tune

anyway. However, slamming down sledgehammer blues behind Janis Joplin, they sounded almost great. She moved in with the band and the rollercoaster started to shudder in anticipation.

She had now been clean for a year. Holed up in the beautiful hippie household, however, where every guitarist had a girlfriend and she was the only one on her own, she began to feel real loneliness. Also, she was one of only two people not doing speed. At last her resolve snapped. Temptation got the better of her and the habit came back.

One thing that she never embraced, being utterly terrified of its unpredictable flashes and psychological squeezes, was LSD. When somebody slipped her an acid-laced drink she made herself vomit rather than tremble her way through a much-feared trip.

That particular idiosyncrasy aside, her own emotional and physical needs coincided conveniently with the prevailing ideas of the hippie community: do what you enjoy and enjoy it while you're doing it. Then, when you've finished doing it, do it again.

Her hard-livin', hard-lovin' exterior endeared her to the Hell's Angels – she would later dedicate an album to them – and they appreciated the competition she provided. Even concern among close friends that she was being made a fool of did not distract her from the riotous arm-wrestling nights with the Angels.

In June 1967 an event happened that changed the lives of Big Brother And The Holding Company, and made an overnight star of their loud, bluesy singer.

The Monterey Festival was an incredible triumph. Playing twice by public demand, they won over the huge audience and made the pages of every national publication with a double-spread to spare and an interest in youth culture. The film made of the festival, *Monterey Pop*, shows a mesmerizing Joplin performance of 'Ball And Chain'. At the end of the song the camera picks up Cass Elliott of The Mamas And The Papas. There is no sound, but you don't need to be told that she is breathing the word 'wow'.

The rollercoaster was moving. Dylan's manager Albert Grossman signed them (significantly, a personal dislike of heroin and the people who use it made him include a clause in the contract stipulating that the deal was off at the first sniff of smack). While the press acclaim reached mayhem level, Janis proved difficult to locate. She was down in Mexico, having an abortion.

The publicity became fame and the fame became madness. Not only was Janis's every move being monitored by the press, she was also receiving free advice. The gist was: that band had *got* to go.

It was certainly true that no-one looked further than Janis when Big Brother played. Her self-destructive streak and pent-up frustration manifested themselves in magnetic performances, her voice spelling out the rage in stuttering phrases punctuated by hair-tossing and fist-clenching. She looked and sounded on the verge of bitter tears.

Nobody was in any doubt about her talents, but the band was getting worse and worse reviews as writers dredged newer and fresher insults from the depths of the thesaurus. The official split came in August 1968 and Janis, guilty as hell, was now a solo singer.

Motivated by a dubious marriage of Southern Comfort and heroin (which she had been taking behind Grossman's back) she put together a band which would variously be called Kozmic Blues, The Janis Joplin Revue and Main Squeeze. Some critics judged them to be absolutely terrible, totally incompatible with Janis's voice, and some depressing audience figures resulted.

Around this time she overdosed on heroin and had to be slapped back to life by two friends.

Her stage performances had become very raunchy, with profanities rife as she spun her lewd stories of sexual abandon. Towards the end of 1969 the Kozmic Blues tour reached Florida, scene of Jim Morrison's notorious audition for *Hair*. Janis, irritated by old-fashioned auditorium rules that prevented people from dancing and enjoying her show, used 'vulgar and indecent language' at a show in Tampa to get her point across. She was fined $200 and her reputation as a far-from-safe bet increased.

She attempted to kick heroin the following month, December, but failed. A few intellectual conversations with her specialist on the nature of obsessive behaviour were not much use in the real world. There was an element of superwoman about her boasts – she shot this, she drank this amount, she slept with all these guys – and her ego was in an eggshell state. On the one hand, she knew she was unique, she was the greatest. On the other hand, she liked to hear people *say* it.

Her reactions to heroin were pretty abnormal. Instead of it draining her sex drive, which is what it's famous for, it seemed to fuel it, and her constitution enabled her to withstand days when heroin was not available. She never shot up before a show, but she definitely did so afterwards, trying to maintain the comfort and warmth of performance. It did not necessarily work. 'On stage I make love to 25,000 people,' she was famous for saying. 'But I'm going home alone.'

In a once-and-for-all effort to come off the drug she went to Brazil for a vacation, where, apart from a motorcycle accident, she had a great time. Clean, in the company of a caring man, seriously happy in Rio, she nevertheless scored smack the minute her plane touched down in Los Angeles. Surrounded by fellow addicts, spongers, leeches and outright thieves, she was hopelessly lost.

Convinced that she was destined to marry the American football star Joe Namath, whom she had met only once, she slumped deeper into a junk morass, emerging only when her best friend and flatmate walked out in disgust.

She split up the Kozmic Blues band shortly afterwards and formed her final and best band, Full-Tilt Boogie. To complete the image she brought a problem of full-tilt alcoholism that saw her seek psychiatric help in the middle of 1970. However, that ended in failure – her analyst only told her what she already knew, that she'd have to change her lifestyle.

What she *did* change was her name. From then on she took to calling herself 'Pearl', the title of a future LP. In Pearl was entrusted the sacred rites of performance – the imploring screech of rejection and betrayal that gave voice to the clenched fists, the bottle by her side, the manic dancing – while Janis got on with the serious business of trying desperately to come off heroin. But, disillusioned with straightness and bored with life, she talked of suicide or, at the very least, a massive re-appraisal of her new drug-free existence. Fascinated by the live-fast die-young legend of blues singer Bessie Smith, she started to consider herself one of the doomed ones, destined never to see 30.

The very real possibility that she would get married – and quit having to always sing the blues – arose in the summer of 1970, during which Janis gave sobriety a chance and appeared to mellow out considerably. But it only took one short separation from her fiancé to bring on the loneliness and she started to mess with heroin again in September, while she was recording what would be her final album. The death of Jimi Hendrix could not shake her out of it; not even dire predictions of moons in Scorpio could shake her out of it. And, following a huge injection of heroin at her Hollywood hotel, she blacked out, fell, hit her head and died sometime in the early hours of 4 October 1970.

The official cause of death was accidental overdose of heroin. It was pointed out that, after months of liberation from the drug, her tolerance level would have been very low.

The tributes were oddly muted. Everyone seems to have seen it coming. Her fellow musicians in the San Francisco community were almost flippant about it, muttering inane platitudes and defending heroin to the end. A typical yeah-well-life-goes-on quote came from The Grateful Dead's organist Ron 'Pigpen' McKernan, himself a disciple of the bottle. He planned a tribute of the most personal kind. 'When I get a few days I'm gonna sit back and get *ripped* on Southern Comfort.'

Unfortunately Pigpen probably did just that, several thousand times over. He died, a shrivelled alcoholic cartoon of his former burly self, of acute liver failure, stomach haemorrhages and internal organ wastage, in March 1973. He was aged 27, exactly the same age in death as Janis Joplin.

# Boy George

The story of how Boy George went from being unequivocally the smash hit of 1983 to the tabloid stooge of 1986 to the sad cabaret artist of 1988 is, if nothing else, a cautionary tale in media manipulation.

George Alan O'Dowd trod the usual path of the true rock 'n' roll rebel/victim. Expelled from school for insubordination, he drifted into an underground London society of drag artists, performance artists and piss artists. He was by no means the most outrageous of them, but he was easily the most talented. His voice was assured and soulful, and he made the transition from merely going to clubs to actually appearing at them when he was snapped up by Malcolm McLaren as co-singer for the band Bow Wow Wow. This was not just a safety measure against the band's teenage singer Annabella quitting, but also a testament to George's striking looks and voice. While he was in Bow Wow Wow he called himself 'Lieutenant Lush'.

Worries over McLaren's influence led to his departure from the band. Besides he had ideas of his own, and soon, with the addition of Jon Moss, Roy Hay and Mikey Craig, an interesting multi-coloured funk-toting four-piece, Culture Club, was conceived. The end result was probably nowhere near as cynical as it looked. But the happy mix of colours and images, to say nothing about the

rumours concerning exactly who if any in the band was gay, got the word around. After a couple of minor hits they had a huge number one success in 1982 with the song 'Do You Really Want To Hurt Me'.

The music press had been courting him for years, since his arrival on the club scene, but when the daily tabloids were faced for the first time with the unashamedly androgynous George, the results were predictable: 'Is It A Her? A Him? Or Is It Neither?' . . . 'Mister (Or Is It Miss?) Weirdo' . . . . He even won the nauseating Nina Myskow Wally Of The Week Award.

When they found out that he was not a freak and indeed had not only a mind of his own but the vocabulary to express it, their claws retracted a good deal. The tabloids even began to interview George, drawing supposedly outrageous quotes from him about how he preferred a cup of tea to sex. He was hardly ever out of the pop gossip columns. The greatest tribute a singer can receive – the *Daily Mirror* Personality Of The Year Award – adorned his mantelpiece for two years in a row.

And all the while hordes of lookalikes – mostly girls, for some reason – followed him in every conceivable fashion style. The records he made with Culture Club – 'Time (Clock Of The Heart)', 'Church Of The Poison Mind', 'Karma Chameleon' –

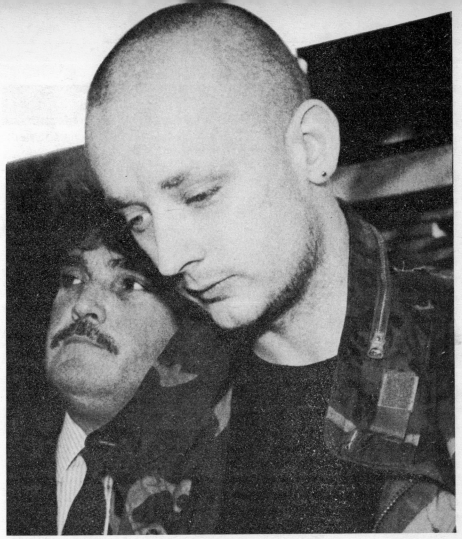

Boy George

outdid each other on the dancefloors and in the charts, and his got-it-flaunt-it style even provoked comment from Princess Margaret ('Who's that over-made-up tart?').

The problem only started when the hits stopped, when George ceased to be the charming vamp in flagrante delicto and began to look vulnerable. By 1986 Culture Club were finished. A string of mediocre records and a blatant lack of number one singles convinced the fickle teenage armies that more exciting thrills lay elsewhere, and George went the way of The Bay City Rollers and Adam Ant before him. Forced to rely exclusively on musical content, he was found wanting. The tabloids hissed a little and sat back waiting for the first mistake.

George had made anti-drug statements in the past and had

persuaded most people that he was much too happy in the high life to mess with narcotics. So it was a genuine shock when the story of his heroin addiction broke in the pages of the *Daily Mirror* in June 1986. The George-as-junkie headlines were given even more lurid life by the fact that the information came from his brother. George had also given an interview to John Blake, writer of the *Mirror*'s pop column, in which he let slip a few indiscretions. Now there was not only a George-on-heroin scandal, there was an O'Dowd-family-at-war scoop as well.

The detective work of Britain's second favourite daily paper was completed by the police, and in the second week of July Boy George was arrested and charged with heroin possession. Later that month he was found guilty, and fined £250.

The nightmare continued. The following month an American musician, Michael Rudetski, aged 27, died at George's Hampstead home. He was to have been a crucial integer in the Boy George comeback plan, being a master of the Fairlight computer. The inquest found traces of heroin and methadone in his blood.

A fortnight later George's friend Marilyn (Peter Robinson), who had been arrested in the same police operation – Operation Culture – was freed on heroin possession charges when the prosecution offered no evidence. The same week saw Radio One DJ's criticizing a song called 'Some Candy Talking', by The Jesus And Mary Chain, because it was 'obviously' about heroin . . .

And still it would not stop. December saw a young unemployed man named Mark Golding, 20, collapse and die, this time at George's flat in Paddington. Again, heroin and methadone were found in his blood.

George disappeared, embraced Buddhism and seemed to be last year's news – used and rejected by his teenage fans in the manner of The Bay City Rollers, Kajagoogoo and Nik Kershaw – when suddenly there came news that he had cleaned up and was ready to stage a comeback.

The comeback was quite surprisingly successful. Releasing a cover version of David Gates's slushy but tuneful 'Everything I Own', George made it back to pole position in the charts. And he had another number one record later in 1987 as a member of 'Ferry Aid'. Now this was ironic. In an effort to raise money for the families of victims of the Zeebrugge ferry disaster, many of whom had won the trip through their competition, *The Sun* set up a supergroup of media alumni, including various EastEnders characters, Page 3 girls, newsreaders and Paul McCartney. And Boy George, who perhaps had reason to hate the tabloid press more than any living human being, accepted the invitation.

Sadly, the comeback faltered on the third or fourth single. It remains to be seen how George O'Dowd will survive the Nineties as a worldly-wise, once-proud musician.

# Jimi Hendrix

On 18 September 1970, Jimi Hendrix, the man who did more than anyone to erase the barriers between black and white music, took several sleeping tablets. The normal dose for the pills he used is one half. Hendrix died after inhaling his own vomit.

The sordid circumstances of his death were a shocking conclusion to a life which, since early 1967, had been phenomenally successful. There are those who remember him as a sad man, perhaps even a manic depressive (a song called 'Manic Depression' appears on his first album, *Are You Experienced*). Eric Burdon of The Animals claimed at the time of Hendrix's death to be in possession of a Hendrix poem which bore traces of a suicide note. Observers at close quarters of his astonishing guitar style could perceive scars on his wrists where the slash marks of the past had attempted to heal.

Like all the best legends, Hendrix's death is much better documented than his birth. The most likely date is 27 November 1942, which would have put him at 27 when he died. The *Rolling Stone* obituary had him as 24. Other publications have suggested that he could have been born in the late Thirties. Whatever the date, the location was Seattle, Washington. He learned to play guitar when he was ten, holding it upside down to compensate for his left-handedness.

After a brief spell in the US Airborne Paratroopers (he was discharged with a back injury) he began to tout for work, playing with The Isley Brothers and Little Richard among others. He quickly won a reputation as a virtuoso, although his stage act was not yet the petroleum-fuelled extravaganza that would make him the smash hit of Monterey and Woodstock.

One night he was discovered playing in a New York club by Chas Chandler, the bassist with The Animals (Chas later went on to manage Slade, thereby embodying the spirit of bathos), and was persuaded to go to England. Chandler was convinced – correctly, as it turned out – that Hendrix's gifts would be better appreciated in the somewhat smaller pond. Returning as a mighty fish in 1967, he had to persuade the Americans that he was one of them and not some crazy English eccentric.

Chandler put him in touch with two English musicians, Noel Redding (bass) and Mitch Mitchell (drums) and the trio began to play gigs as The Jimi Hendrix Experience. The vibe spread through the underground that a new guitar genius was performing all sorts of tricks and making the local heroes look pretty humble.

His wild looks and psychedelic apparel, in tandem with the raw heat of his music, had a sensational effect on audiences. When he played a mundane song like 'Wild Thing' he injected it with a sense of swooping hysteria, played guitar with his teeth, behind his back, between his legs, and eventually actually set fire to the poor instrument to howls of anguish from the fretboard.

He made great records too – 'Hey Joe', 'Purple Haze', 'The Wind Cries Mary', all perfectly in synch with the Summer Of Love and the mindblowing decisions of stoned youth. Europe bowed to him and his success in many countries came literally overnight.

When The Jimi Hendrix Experience played at the Monterey Festival in 1967 it was, incredibly, the band's US debut. They went on stage and immediately defined the event – cool, loud, colourful and ebullient. The lighter fluid came out at the end and up went the guitar. How he must have grinned when The Who passed him on their way to the stage – the world's most notorious destroyers of expensive electronic hardware just about usurped by a frizzy-haired unknown.

His records became more and more adventurous. His third album, *Electric Ladyland*, which achieved some renown quite unconnected with the music when the punters saw the bevy of totally naked women who adorned the cover, was a wonderful tour de force. But there was dissension in the ranks of The Experience, especially from bassist Noel Redding. Hendrix had always written and sung the songs, and was wont to produce them too, but on the cover of *Ladyland* there

was an additional credit to Hendrix for 'direction'. Redding, possibly feeling himself relegated to teaboy status, rebelled and the result was the break-up of the band.

Hendrix formed a new trio, which he called The Band Of Gypsies, with the help of Billy Cox (bass) and Buddy Miles (drums). Gone were the flash pyrotechnics, in came some serious guitar studies. Hendrix only played two concerts with the band. The second was stopped midway through by the man himself, who announced to the audience, 'I'm sorry but we're not quite getting it together', and walked off.

When he died in September in London he had only released four official studio albums. Thereafter a flood of material from the Hendrix vaults saturated the market, a lot of which was woefully half-finished. One track which certainly was finished was the single 'Voodoo Chile' which provided him with his only (posthumous) British number one.

The legend lives in other places than record racks. Everyone who made his acquaintance was flabbergasted by his drug intake. 'He was the heaviest doper I ever met', said Eric Burdon. He did not hide this fact. On trial for possession of heroin in Toronto in 1969, he argued that he had been the dupe of a generous fan. However, he admitted that he had used most drugs. He was acquitted.

Most people's abiding memory of Hendrix is the terrific butchery he perpetrated on 'The Star Spangled Banner' at the Woodstock Festival in

Jimi Hendrix

1969. The story goes that, when he was through hacking at the sacred song of America, the audience were in such stunned catatonic silence that the ensuing applause which can be heard on the record and film of the event had to be edited in later.

His guitar innovations live on in the efforts of more meagre talents and his stage mayhem all looks pretty tame in the cold light of the late Eighties. But while he burned, the music and the smell were of molten gold, and God knows he was a voodoo chile.

# Kit Lambert

Christopher 'Kit' Lambert was an upper-class eccentric, the son of composer and conductor Constant Lambert, who had died of alcoholism at the age of 40. It was said that the son inherited the fatalism of the father and saw a glamour in self-destruction.

Early ambitions to be a film-maker led him to the Railway Hotel in Harrow, accompanied by his assistant Chris Stamp, brother of the actor Terence. That night they were looking for a suitable pop group to make a film about. They saw The Who.

Lambert was intrigued by the band, especially guitarist Pete Townshend's unchannelled aggression and sarcastic intelligence. Seeing a band that looked and sounded the way he felt – uptight, disenfranchized and anarchistic – excited him so much that he and Stamp took over their management.

Lambert's dalliance with The Who was notable for drugs binges – mainly cocaine, which he was introduced to in Los Angeles – and crazy ideas. He was no hustler-manager, but rather a subtle theatrical type, who saw a good move just that bit quicker than anyone

else. When Townshend accidentally banged his guitar off a low ceiling and, in irritation, smashed his coveted instrument to smithereens, Lambert congratulated him and urged him to repeat it in future performances. That, and the Union Jack Mod jackets, was his idea, and he sat back as The Who bore into the heart of America with their dangerous English visions.

However, the band eventually outgrew their manager as first Townshend and then singer Roger Daltrey became more independent, and he was phased out in the early Seventies after some unexplained money losses. Daltrey, asking the band to choose between him and Lambert, sealed the manager's fate. It had been in the balance for a long time – he was practically insane from drugs misuse – and he retreated altogether in 1972.

He bought a small, tumbledown palace in Venice and set about rebuilding it, but most of his money went on scoring drugs and buying the services of pretty young Venetian boys. He called himself Baron Lambert and blitzed himself into heroin unconsciousness. The self-abuse was more satisfying to him when people knew about it, so he made sure people knew about it. Degraded, depressed and deranged, he was made a ward of court in 1978 and persuaded to return to London where his mother could look after him.

In March 1981 he arrived home penniless from a night at a regular haunt, telling his concerned mother that he had been mugged. Later that night he collapsed on the way to the bathroom and fell down the stairs, fracturing his skull. He was on a life support system for three days, after which his family gave the doctor permission to switch it off. Traces of heroin and tuinal (a strong barbiturate) were found in his blood. He was 45.

# Brian Epstein

The young Brian Epstein had been a failure at school, a failure in the army and a failure at acting. That he was suddenly a success at business surprised and delighted his family. He had taken over the record department in the Liverpool branch of the family NEMS store. He built it into one of the North's most important record stores.

Everything was going swimmingly until one day a young man named Raymond Jones came into the store and requested a record that Epstein had never heard of – 'My Bonnie' by Tony Sheridan, notable for being the first Beatles recording. Epstein prided himself on being the first to hear about new records but he was totally unaware of The Beatles, even though they shopped at his store and he had probably seen them and served them.

He resolved to find out more about them. Therefore, one night he went to a local club called The Cavern where he had learned they would be playing. Swiftly locating a quiet corner where the cut of his suit and the brevity of his hair would not be noticed, he checked out The Beatles. He was immediately struck by their casual attitude and attire, and he saw a raw quality to the music that persuaded him to introduce himself to the band. There was something else, too. Epstein, whose sexual relations had been as doomed as his army career, was a homosexual and, to put it bluntly, he fancied them, especially the callow John Lennon, who was quite clearly the loudest, rudest and most outrageous musician he had ever come across.

Impressed by Epstein's enthusiasm and sweet-talked by his acumen, The Beatles agreed to be managed by him and he secured them a record deal with Parlophone after impressing the equally well-spoken George Martin, their future producer.

During the year 1962–63 Epstein became emperor of a recording syndicate that would make him one of the wealthiest figures in rock music. Having seen The Beatles spectacularly hit the upper reaches of the British charts, Epstein busied himself with a host of equally garrulous Liverpudlian wide boys. Gerry And The Pacemakers became history makers when their first three singles all reached number one, a feat unequalled until Frankie Goes To Hollywood in the Eighties. Billy J. Kramer, and his backing group The Dakotas, were an immediate success with a Beatles tune. And Priscilla White, the cloakroom attendant at The Cavern, became a star in the Epstein firmament when he renamed her Cilla Black; and a lifetime of nasal laughs and blind dates had been kickstarted into action. The stable in its entirety was a huge triumph, but it was The Beatles to whom he kept returning.

But the pressures of top-level involvement and the constant worries over 'his' boys and girls meant no sleep for Brian. His personal life was a mess of unfinished business and emotional dead-ends, and the attitude of The Beatles was invariably cold and cutting. However, when a split was mooted, the band stood by him and threatened to break up themselves rather than lose their manager.

Beatlemania reached the States, the Ed Sullivan Show kept juvenile crime off the streets of America for an entire hour, and Epstein's throne sparkled a little brighter with each catchy hit record. When The Beatles were awarded MBEs by Harold Wilson's forward-looking government it was Princess Margaret who asked if MBE stood for Mr Brian Epstein.

However, Epstein was not generally in a laughing frame of mind. His life was a succession of brief encounters punctuated by large intakes of barbiturates and amphetamines. Depression plagued him all day, and insomnia all night and, what was worse, The Beatles were outgrowing him. They had already decided to stop playing live – there was no point, nobody could hear them and only about 40 people could see them – and concentrate on the astonishing music they were getting out of the studio. Epstein's few attempts to influence the band's musical direction ended in humiliation, usually at the hands of Lennon.

After the last live show given by The Beatles, in San Francisco's Candlestick Park, Epstein attempted suicide, stricken by the emptiness of the future. His projects after the Beatles 'retired' were mixed and he took little pleasure in them. Eventually he entered a clinic where his condition was diagnosed as a mixture of depression, exhaustion and insomnia. The pessimism remained even after he left the clinic, and in August 1967 he died of an overdose of sleeping pills. He had been too depressed to remember how many he should take, so he had taken them all.

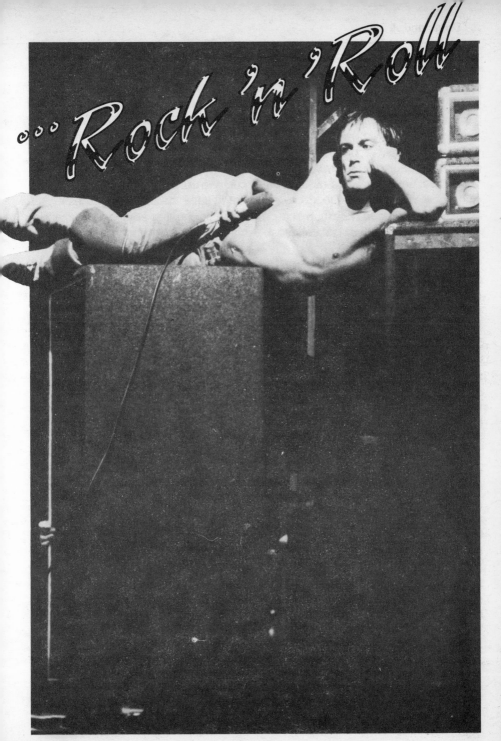

**...Rock 'n' Roll**

Iggy Pop

# Iggy Pop

'I've been spit at, I've been slugged, I've been egged. I've been hit with paper clips, money, cameras, brassieres, underwear, old rags, and with expensive garments and belts and things. I've been hit with, well, a slingshot. Yeah, you just get used to it after a while.'

Play word games with the legend of Iggy Pop and you are liable to arrive at any or all of the following: a self-destructive lunatic; a messiah of sleaze; a poet: a drug-ravaged true survivor (just); a highly articulate and literate artist in the Warholian social realism mould; a drinking buddy of David Bowie's; the man who introduced spitting into the rock 'n' roll context, thereby providing legions of future British punks with a reason to live; the king of the whole damn slum.

Iggy Pop started life in a normal world, born James Osterberg on 21 April 1947. Suffering as a child from severe bronchial asthma he was molly-coddled all the more because of his tiny frame and babyish features. Even today, at 5 ft 1 in (155 cm) and despite the excursions to hell and back, Iggy still looks like a petulant kid.

Rock 'n' roll provided a cool outlet for his exhibitionist talents, and he started off playing drums for a local Michigan school band, The Iguanas, whence came the first half of his nickname.

After avoiding the draft by registering at the army barracks

wearing nothing but a huge erection and claiming to be a homosexual, he formed The Stooges in Detroit in 1968. The line-up was completed by three like-minded square pegs, and they set about their native land with barely-controlled visceral glee.

Jim Morrison of The Doors had opened up whole new avenues of performance with his leather-clad whirling and regaling of the front rows. But Morrison was like a lounge lizard compared to Iggy.

For whereas The Doors perceived themselves as an intelligent and passionate blues group caught up through no fault of their own in distasteful displays of censorship and crowd control, The Stooges, although undeniably a far less popular group, were quite simply a violation of every prevailing rock 'n' roll dictum in the late sixties. Namely, that ye shall sing and play in tune: that the songs ye play shall have some degree of recognizable harmony, however scant and short-lived; and that ye shall at all times cater for and respect your audience, some of whom have paid good money to see you.

On vinyl, which basically amounted to three studio albums between the years 1969 and 1973, plus a live recording from which the passing of time could never wrestle the smouldering sense of violence, what The Stooges played was a fierce slovenly nowhere-bound doomed guerrilla guitar noise. This was laden with some marvellously basic wah wah effects and Iggy's primeval lyrics, most of which were dedicated to the pursuit of that all-important first sexual conquest.

Live, in the flesh, The Stooges were, according to one's taste, one's worst nightmare or wildest dream come to life. While the neanderthals in the band laid down the basic uncompromising gonzo grunge, Iggy turned somersaults, contorted his short-arsed frame into terrible spastic statues, threw himself head first at the stage and screamed into the microphone. When he was done doing that he would slam the mike against his lips until the blood started to flow, scrape the mike stand against his puny body until the blood became a river (screaming all the while) and bang his head on the stage.

Then he would turn on the audience. Spotting a likely victim – preferably a couple – he would jump up on their table and launch horrifying screams of pure hatred in their faces. If this failed to provoke a reaction other than stunned incomprehension he would smash the microphone into his mouth again, and bleed all over the table. As a final party-piece, he would pick up the candle that had stood on the (by now vacated) table, brandish it like Neville Chamberlain, and slowly tilt it so that the hot wax dripped all over his chest.

'Aaaaauuuuuggghhhhh,' he would scream. 'Aaaauuuggghhhhh.' And nobody could be quite sure if it was a cry of pain or simply the next line of the lyrics.

The few people left in the audience would invariably come out with shrewd observations on the lines of, 'If he had done that 200 years ago he'd have been locked up.'

The compulsion that drove Iggy on was also driving him to indulge in drug feasts. Once, showing extraordinary nerve, he entered the offices of Elektra Records and demanded $400 to buy cocaine.

He also emulated Jim Morrison by exposing his genitals on stage, although the authorities never seemed to care what a glorious loser like Iggy Pop got up to in the heat of the moment.

In 1971, when their record company rejected the tapes for their third album, The Stooges combusted. Hooking up with David Bowie, who would become his friend/mentor/lifesaver, Iggy embarked on phase two of The Stooges, even more demented than the first.

Unfortunately The Stooges mark two had a bad time of it, and a soul-destroying American tour so depressed them that confrontation was inevitable. After receiving a beating from a Michigan gang-member at one gig, Iggy went on local radio and challenged the entire gang to come to the evening's show and do their worst.

The recording of the consequences later became a cult album, *Metallic KO*. Despite the atrocious lo-fi production quality one can easily make out the sound of missiles hitting the stage, and Iggy provides a superb running commentary:

'Our next selection tonight for all you Hebrew ladies in the audience is entitled "Rich Bitch" . . . hey, I don't care if you throw all the ice in the world . . . you're paying five bucks and I'm making ten thousand, baby! So screw ya!

'Well, well, ladies and gentlemen, thank you for your kind indulgence. I'm proud to present a song that was co-written by my mother entitled, "I've Got My Cock In My Pocket". One – two – fuck you pricks!

'Aaaah, it'll all be over soon . . . (to female catcalls) I won't fuck you when I'm working. Anybody with any more ice cubes, jelly beans, grenades, eggs, they wanna throw at the stage, c'mon. You paid your money so you takes your choice, you know . . . (Having introduced the band), and let's not forget your favourite well-mannered boy! The singer, let's hear it for the singer! I am the greatest. Thanks for the egg. Do we have any more eggs? Ah, you missed, c'mon, try it again, c'mon! Listen, I've been egged by better than you. Is it time for a riot, girls? Riiiooottt!!!! Lightbulbs too? Paper cups? (Huge crash) – Oh my we're getting violent . . .'

Since the gory glory days Iggy has spent time in a mental hospital, on coke, on smack, on a golf course, and of course on stage. And while his albums aren't quite the devastating pillages of old, he's still the incomparable showman when the lights go down and the amps hit ten.

A footnote: at the 1988 Reading Festival many of the performers, including Meat Loaf and Bonnie Tyler, were assaulted by missiles and bottles of liquid of dubious extraction. Iggy Pop, the most bottled man on the entire bill, did his set to nothing more violent than thunderous applause.

# Alice Cooper

The kid was adamant, 'You suck!' he berated Alice Cooper. Alice, who was born Vincent Furnier, a minister's son from the right side of the tracks (for a change), grinned and could not find it in his heart to disagree. He bent down so that his face was level with the heckler's and began to chant the word 'suck' over and over again.

The kid thought for a moment about his rejoinder.

'You still suck!' he cried.

That was 1970, when the love/hate relationship between America and the phenomenon known as Alice Cooper was at its most ambivalent. Before that they just hated him. Now, even in virtual middle age, they love him.

Alice Cooper was a Frank Zappa acolyte, trained in the use of shock tactics and rock 'n' roll attrition, who eventually outdid his teacher in the projection of disgusting, unnecessarily gross images. If ever a performer deserved hanging it was Alice Cooper. Realizing this, he brought his own gallows on stage with him.

The decision to offend was probably made early on in Furnier's life when he saw The Rolling Stones and what they were getting away with. He formed a band of long-haired reprobates that toured the Michigan area to almost unanimous hostility, playing slab-like angst anthems over which Alice/ Furnier howled his untutored vocals. The name Alice Cooper, he claimed, came from a ouija. The spirit they had contacted wanted to speak to 'Alice Cooper'. When asked who that meant, the spirit replied that it was Vincent Furnier.

In 1969 they met Shep Gordon, who became their manager. The circumstances give some idea of the seriousness of the concept. Alice Cooper and band – they were bracketed as a collective entity, as though so much depravity could not exist in just one man – had reached Los Angeles and were playing a prestige gig at a club there. When Alice was a few songs into the set, something about the menacing leather gear, the whips, the realistic baby dolls that were slaughtered, the live chickens that got molested, the mock hanging of ringleader Alice for all these crimes, the incessant fondling of a morose-looking boa constrictor and the stage blood everywhere inspired the audience en masse to get up and leave. As Gordon put it, 'When I saw 2,000 people walk out on them, I knew I had to manage them.'

Alice admitted that the act was '60 per cent' contrived. His guitarist at the time put his finger on why people were so distressed: 'Towards the end of the act people start to realize that it's not going to stay on stage.'

The basis of the act has always been the execution of Alice Cooper for various sins. This execution has come in numerous forms. The gallows became a guillotine, which in turn became the electric chair. And in order for this to work, it is clear that some suitably nefarious deeds have to be perpetrated first, so that Alice is seen to deserve his punishment. Hence the baby mutilation, the chicken killing, the debauchery.

Yvonne the boa constrictor was his slippery partner in crime, casting her beady eyes over her master's misdemeanors. The Freudian symbolism may have been lost on the less intelligent youth who packed out his shows all through the Seventies, but Alice thought it through. It was inspired theatre and it smacked of danger.

This was because the boundaries of definition between Alice Cooper and Vincent Furnier tended to be obscured once Alice took the stage. Rather than acting out a part – which would have been perfectly acceptable in the bogus glam era – he actually *became* Alice. The crimes were simulated on stage, but they were real in his mind. And although he invariably jokes about it now, it must have been hell on earth coming off stage and finding oneself back in the real world again. No wonder he became a chronic alcoholic.

The real world tried to catch him out. In 1974 a boy in Canada mimicked the mock-hanging act and died. To his credit, Alice dropped the act. But Alice Cooper was becoming a threat to the internal welfare of Vincent Furnier, and in 1977 he sought medical assistance to try to keep his liver. He claimed never to have been sober from 1974 to 1977 and to have regularly put away forty cans of beer a day. His dry-out was a resounding success and Alice became something of a caricature from that point on.

Once people realized that Alice was a put-on the albums stopped doing as well, and Alice was courted as a kind of survivor-celebrity. He was a pretty good golf player, so he got invited to play pro-celeb tournaments. He even appeared on the gameshow, Hollywood Squares, in full make-up.

While the group Kiss – of even less musical know-how and even more schlock appeal – won the appreciation of Alice's erstwhile armies of teenage fans, the man himself mellowed on vinyl and even got a little introspective. The ironic thing is that, had they thought about it, his admirers would have seen far more outrageous success in playing golf with Bob Hope and annoying the heart of America at source, than in singing some loud brazen music to a few thousand already-converted kids.

Alice returned to the stage, with a show that lacked all the menace of the early ones but intensified the humour. Yvonne had been put out to grass, so her place was taken by Arnold (the boa constrictor), if anything an even more natural performer.

And every time he tours all the ingredients are still there. They just seem funnier now (are we all getting older?). The audience knows when to scream in ecstasy and when to scream in terror. There is no trouble. But perhaps Alice thinks back to the days of 1969, to the skin-of-the-teeth getaways:

'A motorcycle gang rushed the stage in Michigan and tried to kill us,' he told a reporter in '69. 'It was great but we felt we had to get out of there.'

# Lou Reed

From the moment he wrote a pop song called 'Heroin' and instantly doomed his then-band The Velvet Underground to a career totally unassisted by radio play, Lou Reed has probably offended more people more frequently than any other contemporary rock musician. His gruesome antics and supposed uncontrolled worship of every malevolent chemical have been exaggerated in the past – not least by the master storyteller himself – but the desire to appal has always been there at the back of his dark, cruelly witty mind.

Like Iggy Pop – perhaps even more so – Lou Reed is a man of extreme intelligence and articulacy. He can talk about himself far better than any writer can write about him. Even the greatest rock writer of them all, Detroit's Lester Bangs, was forced to admit defeat and join his hero in nothing more intellectual than a glorified drinking contest.

An early RCA press release from 1973, the year when Lou Reed had a surprise hit with the single 'Walk On The Wild Side', notes that most people were only then getting to hear Reed's music for the first time. His original band, The Velvet Underground, have without doubt influenced more British bands than anyone else in history. (They all get it hopelessly wrong; if you want to be like The Velvet Underground you jettison *all* influences and do your own thing with a scathing vengeance.) However, by virtue of the fact that Reed was writing, and boasting about having written, songs dealing with such non-Top 40 phenomena as hard drugs, sado-masochism, murder, prostitution and some mysterious den of depravity known casually as The Factory, which turned out to have Warholian connotations, America left them well and truly alone.

They had been formed in 1965 in New York by Reed. Other founder members were his buddy from university, Sterling Morrison on guitar, and a guy named John Cale who played bass but was a classically trained pianist and viola player. Cale had played with legendary underground avant-garde classical composer La Monte Young, doing such crazy things as bringing a plant onstage and screaming at it until it died, and taking part in piano marathons that were supposed to leave you emotionally drained at the end.

Reed himself had been a difficult child and at one stage his parents made him undergo electro-shock therapy for depression. His wealthy, upright family got him into Syracuse University, where he studied English under the poet Delmore Schwartz, a carefree bohemian alcoholic/paranoid whose hatred of pop music Reed later made reference to by dedicating The Velvets' song with fewest lyrics, 'European Son', to him. Lou Reed was by this time a drug taker of cavalier habits. He used heroin overtly and was eventually asked to leave.

After a dead-end job writing imitation pop songs to order for Pickwick Records (his best effort was 'The Ostrich' which introduced a new dance – you put your head on the floor and get your partner to step on it) The Velvets began to take shape. Very coolly at first, not really making any headway, until Andy Warhol turned up one night. This was the night The Velvet Underground's sound proved to be substantially at odds with the requirements of New York's unhip club proprietors. Play that song – 'The Black Angel's Death Song' – one more time, they were told, and you're fired. The next night, they opened their set with it, drawing its spectacular viola rushes and speedy, uneasy lyrics out over 10, 15 minutes. Sure enough they *were* fired.

Warhol moved in, started to direct their career and introduced them to Gerard Malanga, the man with the whip who made The Velvet Underground's early performances a visual as well as an aural thrill. They also met Nico (real name Christa Paffgen) who was a European model of quite disconcerting beauty who had had a child by the French actor Alain Delon. In the end scant details emerged about her except that she was German, had appeared in Fellini's *La Dolce Vita* and had a stunning Teutonic whisper of a singing voice. Reed sat down to write some songs for her. (Nico eventually came to live in England, having left The Velvets in 1968, and made several classic solo albums. A committed heroin addict, she died in 1988 on holiday in Spain. Death was attributed to heart failure.)

The first Velvet Underground LP was only noted at the time (1967) for its weird cover – with the picture of an unpeeled banana. It was a Warhol idea and he signed it just in case people did not get the picture. Unpeeled sleeves are now almost priceless.

The music disappeared without trace. American music in 1967 meant Jefferson Airplane and The Grateful Dead, both of whom Reed loathed, and songs of vague, half-baked brotherly love. The black core of authenticity which featured in all The Velvets' songs of the street was the exact antithesis of the San Francisco hey-man-like-what's-happenin' types. In typically deadpan style, the LP came accompanied with its own bad reviews on the gatefold sleeve.

Their second LP, *White Light/White Heat*, was, if anything, even less enthusiastically received by the pop populace, although critics in certain quarters saw a vulnerable beauty to its spewing feedback-toting contents. Its longest and scariest song, 'Sister Ray', was a 17-minute epic the like of which nobody had ever heard: to an increasingly frazzled backing noise of organ, guitars and barely audible drums Reed recounts a tale of oral sex, murder, drag queens, heroin injection and orgies of sex and violence. The casual listener might just be able to decipher Reed's flat voice mentioning something about 'sucking on his ding-dong'. It was the ultimate one-take song.

The Velvet Underground became a marginally less interesting band in 1968 when Reed fired Cale, and the LPs they made until their combustion in 1970 were highly melodic, almost spiritual in tone.

Reed's solo career got off to an inauspicious start with a decidedly ropey eponymous album. But his 1972 effort, the David Bowie-produced *Transformer*, was a great success and all of a sudden Reed found himself catapulted into the front rooms of the western world on delivery of a hit single, 'Walk On The Wild Side'. The song was a memorable juxtaposition

of a suitably languid bass line and a résumé of events at Andy Warhol's Factory. The people mentioned in the song – Holly, Candy, Jackie and Joe – were erotic freaks on the periphery of the art scene. To judge by Reed's song they were already lost souls by the time they made it to New York.

The song was a big hit in Britain, winning constant airplay, which was a source of much mirth in the hip press – the folks at the BBC couldn't be too au fait with US slang, it was said, or else they would surely have baulked at the line, 'But she never lost her head/ Even when she was giving head'. And if nothing else, at least 'Walk On The Wild Side' got feminine shaving mentioned in a song for the first time.

The sight of Lou Reed was still something that the public at large were not adequately geared for, however, and the image was becoming more and more uncompromising. The odd transvestite reference in the song was compounded by Reed's propensity for eyeliner. In the early Seventies he and David Bowie (and to a lesser extent Brian Eno of Roxy Music) crossed a great many barriers with regard to androgyny in rock.

Bisexuality fascinated Reed, just as it did Bowie, and, like Bowie, Reed liked to write about it. And, like Bowie, he was married. The edges blur on many of his songs; it's not clear if the relationship he is alluding to at a given point is straight or gay. He relished the confusion, and in interviews he slipped in additional teasers, intimating that the two topics that interested him most were devil worship and suicide.

The awful pain of listening to the entire contents of *Berlin*, the 1973 album on which Reed's concerns with self-destruction, dope, bad sex and suicide gelled horrifically, tends to detract from its more straightforward, *musical* strengths. Listening to Reed recount the squalid tale of Caroline, the beautiful junkie slut whose artistic aspirations die like butterflies by the Berlin Wall, and her loser husband Jim, is an unsettling, almost voyeuristic experience. As the couple's kids are taken away by the authorities and Caroline kills herself in desperation, the listener concedes that this is the single most depressing record ever made. This record probably killed off the cosy drag image, showing Reed to be an expert on more than just matters chemical.

The album also saw the nervous breakdown of its producer, Bob Ezrin, who made the terrible mistake of trying to keep up with Reed. His habits steered him towards total collapse.

The brilliance of *Berlin* was not widely acknowledged. In fact, the record was savagely panned for its indulgence (how can one write about suicide and *not* be indulgent?) and the attacks took personal form. Most writers agreed that Reed's lowlife trawls were a bit distasteful. Well, sure. And the album's closing song is not called 'Sad Song' for nothing. But, one of them conceded, at least it was good to see Lou writing about heterosexuals again.

One of the problems people had with the record – and others made by Lou Reed – was the attitude of the artist. His famous deadpan drawl, a 'monotone of nuances' as one writer put it, adopts a dispassionate, purely journalistic stance. Not pro, not anti, just *there*. And for him to paint a musical picture of a crumbling marriage and a decaying life in which hopes of reconciliation and rejuvenation are not even entertained was clearly to invite antagonism.

More ill feeling was encountered on the *Berlin* tour. An overriding sense of violence became the reality of personal assaults, as Reed laid his menacing street voodoo on the audiences. His fans, recently swayed to the cause in the wake of 'Walk On The Wild Side' and certainly in no sober state to consider Reed as a bona fide artist, behaved like idiots and thugs, believing that this was expected of them. As for the man himself, stage performances became extraordinary exercises in self-loathing. All done up in whiteface, lipstick, eyeliner and leather, he stalked the stage as his second-degree heavy metal band played havoc with the subtleties of 'Heroin' and 'Sweet Jane'.

The subtext suggested that Lou was lost and sure enough the image altered drastically in a matter of weeks. The hair was shaved off to accommodate a Swastika clipped into the remaining blonde thatch; he looked pipe-cleaner thin and he didn't blink – not once.

1974 saw him take up with the notorious Rachel, a half Mexican transsexual whose undeniable delectability was slightly undermined by the quarter-inch stubble that shadowed his/her face. A lifetime of reformatories and prisons made Rachel the perfect companion for Reed. The resulting tour, during which he promoted his *Sally Can't Dance* album (the reason Sally couldn't dance was because she was dead, of a drug overdose), had Reed peroxide his hair, put on some nail varnish, shed another perilous few pounds, highlight the iron cross and depress every critic who saw the shows.

Typically, the critics' wrath was compensated for by the antics of the dumb Quaalude quorum who yelped their way through 'Heroin', lazily overlooking its lyrical skill and assuming it to be something between an artist's tribute to his muse and an ideal for living.

The whole sorry business reached its stultifying conclusion in December 1974. 'Heroin' became a party piece, a vehicle for a true moronic showbiz gimmick in which Reed produced a syringe, wrapped the microphone cord tight around his arm to bring up a vein, and simulated the act of injection. At least it was *assumed* he simulated it. Later Reed claimed never to have shot heroin, although the methamphetamine in his bloodstream presumably didn't get there by accident.

There was deep concern about his welfare. Sometimes he was violent and unhinged. Other times he just did not

Lou Reed

seem to be there at all. Talking backstage with Mick Jagger at a Madison Square Garden gig, he was asked if he had ever played there before. 'How the fuck should I know?' he replied.

In 1975 Lou Reed shocked, flummoxed and appalled his few straggling disciples with the release of an album ominously entitled *Metal Machine Music*. The reviews of *Berlin* were as nothing compared to the outbursts of sheer visceral hatred directed at the 64 minutes and four seconds of *Metal Machine*.

Lou doesn't exactly play on it; no-one does. And he doesn't sing; there aren't any words. What you get is just over an hour of shrieking electronic fury in the form of a non-stop drone, a couple of bleeps and the odd motif of a tune. The album was not, it must be stressed, played for laughs. Nor was there a surfeit of rib-tickling when Reed acolytes purchased the record in their local shop. Copies were returned in droves and RCA, who had actually been thinking of releasing it on their classical Red Seal label, were forced to make an apology. Reed defended the album in strong terms, calling it 'the closest I've ever come to perfection; it's the only record I know that *attacks* the listener'. It certainly attacked the poor wretches who forked out the hard-earned for it and sat wondering if maybe there had been a fault at the pressing plant.

He also indignantly refuted rumours that sides three and four were merely sides one and two backwards,

something suggested by the fact that each side lasted exactly 16 minutes and one second.

This whole question of recording, for posterity and judgment by one's peers, what seems at the time to be a good idea typifies Lou Reed's career. It is a career unparalleled in its variety (only Marlon Brando's acting career, with its troughs of garbage and peaks of genius, comes close), and the zenith and the nadir are so far apart that one forgets what each looks like and they keep getting mistaken for each other. Now, years later, as the act of a madman, or an incorrigible drug fiend, or simply an artist who wasn't very together, *Metal Machine Music* makes sense. Once you have been written off as a completely unreliable chemist's shop there isn't much you can do to shock people. Rock 'n' roll as a two-fingered gesture is quite often the only recourse.

Lou wasn't finished.

After a brace of decent rock 'n' roll returns to form, he made a live album called *Take No Prisoners*. There aren't many live albums like it, certainly not in the rock context. Lenny Bruce fronting The Doobie Brothers might have made something similar. Amid a torrent of foul language and off-the-cuff observations he takes verbal revenge on the press.

Ironically, the two critics he chooses to badmouth, Robert Christgau of *Village Voice* and John Rockwell of the *New York Times*, were actually fans. But neither had been too chuffed with Lou's vinyl indiscretions in the past, and both had laid into *Metal Machine Music*. Reed asks rhetorically what Christgau gets up to in bed and wonders if he might be a 'toefucker'. Rockwell fares a little better, although Reed gives him a hard time for calling him 'Mr Reed' in his articles.

He starts to sing 'Walk On The Wild Side' and comes in on the wrong beat. 'I have no attitude without a cigarette,' he says. 'I'd rather die of cancer than be a faggot. That wasn't an anti-gay remark. Coming from me that's a compliment. It's like going to bed with a brontosaurus, it's out of style.'

In another selected outburst he declares, 'I do Lou Reed better than anybody, so I thought I'd get in on it.'

It was once pointed out that the quicker you say 'Lou Reed' the closer it sounds to 'lurid'. Fair enough, he has documented activities and personalities that less honest writers would gratefully leave alone. But anyone who can sum up a character, a philosophy, a life force, maybe even an entire generation in one line has got to be considered a major contributor to the human controversy. For the record, that line goes, 'You know some people ain't got no choice and they can never find a voice to talk with that they could call their own, so the first thing that they see that allows them the right to be, they follow it. You know it's called . . . bad luck.'

# David Bowie

In April 1971 a strange record hit the shops of Britain. Not overwhelmingly strange in content, although the music was forbidding and dark and the lyrics showed a strong fascination with mental illness. What was strange about it was the cover. It was a photo of a man in a dress.

To be precise, it was a photo of David Bowie in a dress, lounging on a couch with one hand stroking his hair and the other holding a playing card. The dress was one of six that he had bought from a hip London boutique. The album was called *The Man Who Sold The World* and it was not a huge commercial success.

The music world had already heard of David Bowie by 1971. As a veteran

of various R&B and mod bands during the mid-Sixties he had earned some renown as an okay singer and fair saxophonist. He had also had a top five hit in 1969, with the weird death-in-the-capsule song 'Space Oddity'.

By the time the newspapers caught up with him in 1971–72 Bowie had tired of the obscurity in which his life threatened to remain. On the wings of a spectacular publicity campaign spearheaded by his manager Tony De Fries, Bowie was urged to look, talk, act and dress like a star. Eventually, pop music being what it is, he became a star. The outrage, however, the love of the good scam and the memorable quote, they had all been implanted several years previously . . .

David Robert Jones was born in January 1947 in Brixton. A member of a large, interweaving family, he was attached as a child to his half-brother Terry, who was ten years older than him.

The family was noted for the streak of schizophrenia which paralysed first David's grandmother, then his aunt and finally his half-brother. Fears that he too may be afflicted with the illness led him to reject his family at the first opportunity; he has also claimed to be terrified of psychiatrists.

At the age of 15 David had a fight with a school friend in which the muscles in his left eye were irreparably damaged. The pupil would not close, and to this day his eyes are oddly unmatched: one is blue, the other grey and the pupils vary substantially in size.

A more lurid schooldays escapade concerns his early sexual experiences. 'It didn't really matter who or what it was with,' he has said, 'as long as it was a sexual experience. So it was some very pretty boy in class in some school or other that I took home and neatly fucked on my bed upstairs.'

David had been playing guitar at school and had taken saxophone lessons from the noted jazz saxophonist Ronnie Ross (who would much later play the sax break on Lou Reed's 'Walk On The Wild Side', a Bowie co-production). In 1962 David joined his first group, The Kon-Rads and had a preliminary bash at song-writing.

Leaving them to join The King Bees, one of whom, George Underwood, was the same chap who had injured David's eye in the school playground, he started out on an R&B imitation trip, singing in a pseudo-black style. That was exactly what The Rolling Stones were doing, and people were certainly taking notice. A record deal resulted, although the song itself was a flop.

Linking up with a budding authentic R&B combo called The Manish Boys he continued to pursue the American dream, and built up a strong rapport with his audiences. Dominating the group right from the off, he also took care of the interviews, one of which was with Cliff Michelmore on 'Tonight'. David was defending the civil rights of long-haired men everywhere: 'For the last two years we've had comments like "Darling" and "Can I carry your handbag" thrown at us and I think it just has to stop now.'

It was with The Manish Boys that his 'camp' stage act started to alienate the provincials in the audience, and quick exits from greaser ballrooms were often necessary.

Eventually, the failure of Manish Boy vinyl to set the world alight precipitated David's departure and in 1965 he joined a viable professional recording outfit called The Lower Third. His split from them in January 1966 was brought about by a failure amongst group members to realize who exactly was the star of the show. David Jones became David Bowie and from now on any people he played with would be very definitely his backing band.

A few mod excursions came and went, as did several record deals, until at last the Bowie composition 'Space Oddity', the story of Major Tom's hassles with the circuits, struck oil in 1969, the year of Neil Armstrong. The song was a huge success at the time and an even bigger one when it was re-released in 1975.

The songs Bowie was now writing were entertaining themes of darkness, evil and insanity. Scared of LSD because of its links with mental instability and schizophrenia, and living in close proximity to Terry, he started to genuinely experiment with his lyrics, asking huge, unanswerable questions and coming up with great responsive shrugs like: 'I'd rather stay here/With all the madmen/For I'm quite content/They're all as sane as me.'

That song, 'All The Madmen', was one of the tracks on the controversial-cover album, *The Man Who Sold The World*.

By now Bowie was married, to Angie Barnett, a fiercely free-thinking American girl whose curriculum vitae included her expulsion from college for having an affair with another female student and the intriguing fact that when she and David Bowie met for the first time, they were both sleeping with the same person.

In Angie, Bowie had a willing partner in crime and slowly the great Bowie hype plan for immediate stardom and world domination started to gain momentum. The whole thing gelled when Tony De Fries came on the scene, a man whose ruthless ambition matched Bowie's own, and whose business acumen would be the perfect counterpart to the artist's rock 'n' roll excesses.

The first hint that this might be a brilliantly productive partnership came on a trip to New York in 1971. Urged by De Fries at all times to think 'star', Bowie travelled first-class and behaved like Mae West after a particularly anxious hour in front of a mirror. He got to meet Elvis, Lou Reed and Iggy Pop, and elements of all these diffuse performers would be meshed together in the single most ingenious musical creation of the Seventies, Ziggy Stardust.

Ziggy would be an alien who comes to earth and is hailed as a rock star. The album which came out in 1972, *The Rise And Fall Of Ziggy Stardust And The Spiders From Mars*, was an undeniably fine record, but it was the concerts that were thrown to promote it which secured, then and for all time, David Bowie's reputation as one of the most extraordinary characters in rock 'n' roll.

Before all that, however, one more media master-stroke was needed.

In an interview with *Melody Maker* David Bowie became the first rock star to admit to being gay. 'I'm gay and always have been,' he said, 'even when I was David Jones.' Asked why he wasn't wearing his woman's dress, he sighed, 'Oh dear, you must understand that it's not a woman's, it's a man's dress.' The article was published with a Bowie song title as its headline: 'Oh You Pretty Thing'. All of a sudden every journalist in the land wanted to talk to David Bowie.

The Ziggy tour electrified Britain. Working as a bizarre intergalactic duo, Bowie and his lead guitarist, former Hull municipal gardener Mick Ronson, played off each other, Bowie simulating fellatio on Ronson's guitar, Ronson pouting away like a coquettish French maid.

The tour wound up at the Royal Festival Hall, at a Save The Whale benefit. The ensuing press was ecstatic. There was just one thing – De Fries had denied the press access to Bowie for the foreseeable future. He was, after all, just too big a star to be messing around with hacks, right? The public were left starved of Bowie so that the merest hint of activity was liable to lead to mass hysteria. Meanwhile Bowie was beginning his jet set period, being driven everywhere in limos, protected by gigantic bodyguards. The product was being marketed, and the market was drooling in expectation.

Anything with Bowie's name on it would do. Career-reviving Bowie productions for Mott The Hoople, Lou Reed and Iggy Pop kept him busy during 1972. On a gruelling tour of the States, during which he collapsed with exhaustion, the line between Ziggy and the frail, artistic performer whose job it was to 'play' him every night was beginning to blur.

After a disastrous show at Earl's Court and a monstrously long British tour, Bowie made the following announcement at Hammersmith

Odeon on Independence Day, 1973: 'This has been one of the greatest tours of our lives, and of all the shows on this tour this particular show will remain with us the longest because not only is it the last show in the tour, but it's the last show we'll ever do.' The audience, stunned and hurt, launched into a spontaneous wail of 'Noooooooo!!!!' and some even began to cry.

Bowie was not retiring as such. He was merely getting rid of one of the problems. Unable to be totally sure who was David Bowie and who was Ziggy, he killed the alien off. The guest list at the party after the show gives some indication of the status that the Bowie phenomenon had attained – the Jaggers, the McCartneys, Barbra Streisand, Tony Curtis, Ryan O'Neal, Peter Cook and Dudley Moore, Elliott Gould, they all came to pay their respects to the prettiest star of all.

'I became Ziggy Stardust,' he said later. 'Everybody was convincing me that I was a Messiah . . . I got hopelessly lost in the fantasy.'

Bowie, deadened by years of hassles with musicians, did not baulk at sacking the Spiders From Mars, his backing band, when the tour finished. He kept Mick Ronson, had a quick rethink, and entered the next phase, the horror of 1984 and the apocalypse that caused it.

The album that resulted, *Diamond Dogs* (on which Bowie usurped Ronson and played the guitar parts himself), is an edgy, almost visual document in music of Orwell's famous novel. The show that promoted it was a theatrical tour de force. The cityscape around him may have been disintegrating, but he was creating new music, new drama. But there was one ingredient that was making the trip an especially risky one.

Shattered from his ridiculously heavy schedule and the physical exertions on stage, Bowie began to use cocaine. People around him noticed stark changes in personality when he was taking coke – and he seemed to become hooked pretty quickly.'I had more than a passing relationship with drugs,' he said later. 'Actually I was zonked out of my mind. One winter's day, three days before Christmas, a friend pulled me over to the mirror and said, "Look at us both . . . if you continue to be the way you are at the moment you'll never see me again, you're not worth the effort." After that I locked all my characters away forever.'

The drug-ravaged Bowie was now a gaunt, hollow-cheeked stick insect for all to see. He was subsequently to describe the years 1975–76 as 'probably the worst year or year and a half of my life'. Ironically, some of his most compelling music dates from precisely that period, with the 1976 album Station To Station being a strong contender for his best ever album.

He had broken free of De Fries in early 1975, sick of the constant pressures of stardom, and De Fries got one of the most lucrative pay-offs in legal history. There was even a proviso that De Fries heirs could claim royalties from sales of Bowie albums made between 1972–82 in the future from Bowie heirs. But David Bowie had finally bought freedom.

One of the first things to do to clean his act up was move out of Los Angeles, the city he had inhabited since Diamond Dogs. Calling it 'the most vile piss-pot in the whole world . . . the scariest movie ever written', he suggested in 1980 that the place 'should be wiped off the face of the earth'.

With the help of his aide/manager Corinne Schwab and his friend and rival in drug overload, Iggy Pop, Bowie underwent something of a transformation on his 1976 'Thin White Duke' tour, coming across as a cool Sinatra type, aloof from his audience, bathed in white light. The shows had a strong European flavour, influenced at least as far as the set was concerned, by impressionist film-directors and surrealist painters. He was also getting heavily into Brecht, the German dramatist, and, more disturbingly, architects of Nazi propaganda such as Albert Speer, who had designed the Nuremberg Stadium in such a way that Hitler's position in the centre would be highlighted by white light.

Around this time Bowie was invoking Hitler in interviews, at first with tongue firmly wedged in cheek ('I think I might have been a bloody good Hitler. I'd be an excellent dictator. Very eccentric and quite mad'). But then it got a bit more serious. 'I believe very strongly in fascism. People have always responded better under a regimental leadership.' He also called Hitler 'one of the first rock stars'. And Britain, he believed, 'could benefit from a fascist leader. After all, fascism is really nationalism.'

The nightmare intensified in May 1976 when Bowie arrived in London for some Wembley shows. Emerging at Victoria Station dressed in a brown shirt, he was ushered into a black Mercedes Benz. He stood up to greet the people who had flocked to see him and was snapped in mid-wave. The photograph which resulted was damning and explicit – there, in all his puerile trash rock glory, was David Bowie giving the Nazi salute. The image lingered for many years, despite protestations that it was only a harmless wave, and that anyway it was all done with irony, and besides it was during a very mixed-up period of his life, and what's so bloody serious about a bit of rock 'n' roll theatre anyway?

Then Bowie went to live in Berlin, where he recorded his *Low* album and worked on Iggy's *The Idiot*. He took inspiration from the Berlin Wall, did some shopping and sailed around the various Strassen without being recognized. The *Low* album, perfectly titled, stands as his most depressive work ever. Some of the songs he could not even bring himself to write lyrics for. The reviews were scathing. One writer called it 'an act of purest hatred and destructiveness', another 'Hunnish'.

In 1980 the stormy and irregular marriage between Bowie and his wife Angie ended in divorce. It was an acrimonious business, with great amounts of money being at stake, as well as the custody of their child, Zowie (he later expressed the understandable wish to be addressed as 'Joe').

Angie had been displaying signs of erratic behaviour for a while. She had attacked her lover, guitarist Keeth (sic) Paul, and attempted suicide a couple of times. David told the court she was an unfit mother and a drug addict. In the end she got a large settlement and he got custody of his son.

In 1983 he returned to the arena with the upbeat, optimistic *Let's Dance* album and a string of sell-out concerts. The image was scrupulously clean, the conversations peppered with tributes to his son and he revealed that he went to bed at ten and got up at six.

In January 1985 his half-brother Terry committed suicide by throwing himself under a train near the mental hospital where he had been living on and off since 1969. Bowie sent a message to the funeral. It read: 'You've seen more things than we could imagine, but all these moments will be lost, like tears washed away by the rain.'

The David Bowie of the late Eighties is not, it has to be said, a very interesting figure. At Live Aid he delighted the audience by dedicating his song 'Heroes' to the children of the world, and by hamming it up on video in a duet with Mick Jagger of the old

Motown classic 'Dancing In The Streets'. But the dangerous charges of the past are not working any more, and the songs are not the mysteries of the inner sanctum that made, say, *Hunky Dory*, such a great record. Drug-free, sane and happy, David Bowie sings his old songs in concert now as if they were written by a slightly wacky young nephew. See what you make of this, he smirks, as 'Rebel Rebel' starts up, reminding us of what a wide and mighty ravine separates art and artifice.

# Frank Zappa

Some day, somewhere, at one of the more left-field polytechnics perhaps, or at a Californian Child Psychology Seminar, someone is going to write a paper on the bizarre phenomenon of rock stars giving their hapless progeny ridiculous names. To be sure, there is no shortage of material for the thesis. Zowie Bowie would expect to feature heavily, as would Rolan Bolan, Zak Starkey and Dandelion Richards. The daughter of Bob Geldof and Paula Yates, Fifi Trixibelle, will surely not be ignored.

But for sheer genius in the field of nonsensical nomenclature the man to whom all encyclopaedic roads invariably lead is Frank Zappa, the man with the strange rectangular beard that never seems to move, the man with the weird smutty lyrics, and the only man ever to have written a song about dental floss.

His four children have had to brave the playing fields of America with the names Moon Unit, Dweezil, Ahmet Emuukha Rodan and Diva Thin Muffin Pigene.

In the world of Frank Zappa, such behaviour is completely natural. He has been accused on many occasions of being abnormal, to which he has said the following: 'If we consider what most people accept as normal behaviour in America today – stuff like Video Christian fanaticism, drug abuse, enthusiasm for tennis or other activities which cause orange hair, then I definitely qualify for abnormality.'

A 20-year-plus career of unique musical diversity which has seen him embrace everything from doo-wop to jazz to disco to rock 'n' roll to chamber music has divided the record-buying public right down the middle. For every yawning cynic who ajudges him to be, in the words of óne of his records, 'only in it for the money', there is another prepared to defend him to the death as *the* most inventive and morally sound performer in rock history.

He's certainly a one-off. Extraordinarily prolific, he's made over 40 albums, gone through countless backing musicians, had innumerable scrapes with the forces of orthodoxy, patronized a host of unmarketable fringe freak figures, customized a facial look that perfectly suits his

Frank Zappa and friend

fidgety, intense music, satirized anything that had a remotely inflated view of itself, and travelled a lyrical line that has never veered from its extreme proximity to the knuckle.

And when the rock 'n' roll charade gets a little too wearisome for him, he'll usually be found hanging out with some internationally famous orchestra.

Frank Zappa was born in Baltimore, Maryland, in 1940. Starved of access to music until his late teens, his early songwriting efforts were so off the wall that no record company would go near him. He resorted to making porno tapes for stag movies at his own recording studio. This little ruse ended when he was busted by two undercover cops. Asked by them to make a 'hot' tape, Zappa got a young female companion to join him in a staged bedside romp, complete with suggestive sound effects and provocative dialogue. He was arrested for 'conspiracy to propagate pornography, lust and lascivious attitudes'. Although he managed to stay out of jail, the 24-year-old Zappa was forbidden to be in the presence of women less than 21 years old unless there was a 'responsible' person in the vicinity.

Around this time, Zappa founded The Mothers Of Invention. The Mothers, as they were called until record company pressure prevailed ('mother' is recognized American shorthand for the sort of bloke who . . . well anyway . . . ), were a motley bunch of strange and wonderful musicians playing a hybrid of rock and freeform jazz before the term jazz-rock had been coined. Indeed, the whole genre had scarcely been defined. Audience reactions therefore were vehement and to the point. Some loved them, some loathed them.

One of the most difficult aspects of The Mothers' shows for the audience to get a hold on was the Zappa personalized theatre of the absurd. All manner of props featured in the performances – stuffed giraffes filled with whipped cream, primed to explode all over the front rows, phallic sticks of salami, life-size dolls. One night Zappa spotted some uniformed Marines in the audience. This was during the most harrowing days of the Vietnam War, the 'hell-no-we-won't-go' phase, when Marines were widely reviled. Reaching for a life-size human doll, he invited the Marines to give the rest of the audience some idea of the way 'our boys' were treating the 'gooks' out in Nam. They proceeded to demonstrate with relish. Or as Zappa put it, 'they ripped the shit outa that doll'.

When Zappa followed up the freeform explorations with a kind of electronic chamber music, audience hostility reached its height. Not only was the new music alienating a lot of young people, but Zappa's refusal to offer glib statements on world issues or the state of the revolution, allied to his fierce anti-drug stance, was bound to end in a showdown. Surprisingly, it happened in London.

England possibly had higher hopes of Frank Zappa than even the States.

Revered as a true anti-establishment figure and paragon of lewd virtue (an early British publicity shot had featured a baleful Zappa sitting astride a toilet), he was engaged by the politically active students at the London School Of Economics to give a morale-boosting talk on the Haight-Ashbury scene, and maybe give some hints. Instead, he sat onstage with legs crossed and merrily took the mickey out of the achingly sincere students.

'How seriously do you take yourself and your music?' he was asked. 'Not enough to be dangerous,' he smirked 'twixt Zapata moustache and rectangular beard. They tried a different tack. Was he, in all honesty, doing all he could to help bring down the Establishment? 'I'm in favour of being comfortable,' he grinned. It was made painfully clear that he intended to be no spokesman for any generation. As he said himself: 'Don't call me a hippie. I'm a freak, not a hippie.'

And freaks, being freaks, like to chew the fat with other freaks. Zappa formed his own record company, Straight/Bizarre, and gathered together some of the less cohesive citizens of US musical society. There was the spell-binding wit and basso profundo genius of Don Van Vliet, alias Captain Beefheart, inarguably one of the most staggering artistic talents of the last 30 years. Zappa was soon to find that the Captain did not take kindly to being marketed as an amiable fruitcake.

After a monumental falling-out

Beefheart began a campaign of anti-Zappa propaganda, calling him a 'sham', a 'bum', and 'the most disgusting character I have ever encountered'. Zappa replied by claiming to have discovered Beefheart and that the good Captain ought to give a little credit where it was due. Zappa's excellent production of Beefheart's 1969 masterpiece *Trout Mask Replica* left the Captain less than impressed: 'He was asleep at the controls, man. He was like a switchman with Parkinson's disease.' The two of them subsequently made up and recorded together again.

Then there was the all-girl band The GTO's (it stood for Girls Together Outrageously), a collection of groupies. And there was the shell-shocked street poet Wild Man Fischer. Fischer had seen the inside of a few mental hospitals before Zappa ran into him and immediately saw inherent raw beauty in the tuneless street singing. One listen to Fischer's Zappa-produced album *An Evening With Wild Man Fischer* will confirm that his thought processes were, if not hanging by a thread, moving along a disturbingly vertiginous plane. He too is said to be deeply unhappy about the way Zappa treated him.

The only Straight/Bizarre act to go from strength to strength was Alice Cooper, who sucked up the Zappa tactics like a Hoover, added the odd snake and laughed all the way to the blood bank.

In 1970 Zappa began work on a musical film called *200 Motels*. A story of his band's adventures in the imaginary town of Centreville, it was notable for early acting performances by Ringo Starr and Keith Moon. The music from the film, scored for rock group and orchestra, was scheduled to receive an important airing at London's Royal Albert Hall in early 1971. The Royal Philharmonic Orchestra was booked to assist the Zappa personnel in the playing of the *meisterwerk*. If successful, the event was expected to totally vindicate Zappa's overbearing self-promotional devices and catapult him to the forefront of serious modern American music.

Just then, somebody at the Albert Hall read the lyrics of *200 Motels*. It is difficult, in retrospect, to say for sure which lyrics in particular swung the balance against Zappa. Certainly the pornographic libretto to the heroine's early-evening calisthenics ('Half A Dozen Provocative Squats'), which managed to mention four previously taboo bodily functions in one verse, must have raised the odd eyebrow. And they are sure to have taken umbrage at 'Shove It Right In'. However, if there remained one solitary doubt in the minds of the trustees about Zappa's plans vis-à-vis their esteemed hall, it vanished upon one perusal of 'Penis Dimension'. The gig was, as rock parlance would have it, 'blown out', and quick.

In a memorable statement, the spokesman for the Albert Hall accused Zappa of 'hiding his filth behind the façade of the Royal Philharmonic'. He was a pedlar of 'filth for filth's sake'. Zappa replied that there was more filth to be heard on daytime pop radio. Certainly pornographic lyrics have always been an integral part of Zappa's work, and it's hard to deny their shock value. Zappa invariably defends them as witty and provocative in a positive sense.

The leaning towards classical music had been manifesting itself in another way – he had worked out a form of conducting through facial signs and gestures, designed to help the musicians play his complex, multi-speed music. It was perfectly in the nature of things for him to put down his guitar and conduct. Then, one night at London's Rainbow Theatre, he got a chance to conduct from the orchestra pit . . .

His connections with groupies had won him quite a reputation. As well as championing the notorious GTO's he also claimed to have married a groupie ('and an excellent groupie, too'). By late 1971 there was a prevailing feeling that, should a budding groupie approach the swarthy rock star, the two of them could probably work out some sort of arrangement. One such girl made the mistake of inviting her boyfriend along to the Zappa gig at the Rainbow, and spent the entire show informing the poor chap about what she would like to do to Zappa in the privacy of the star's dressing-room. The aggrieved beau climbed onstage and despatched Zappa to the depths of the orchestra pit, whence he was

rescued with concussion and a broken leg. The assailant went to prison; Zappa learned to steer a wheelchair.

His profile since those halcyon days has inevitably diminished. No longer a prominent freak, merely a prolific one, he has nevertheless become something of an authority on the subject of censorship. Fervently on the side of the artist, he was shocked into verbosity with the advent of the Parents' Music Resource Center in the mid-Eighties. The PMRC was spearheaded by Tipper Gore, the wealthy and influential wife of the Democrat Senator, Albert Gore. Together with the equally wealthy and equally influential members of the group she ran a campaign against all references to 'sex, violence, drugs and satanism' in rock music, and drew up a shortlist of persistent offenders. Most of these were fairly mindless purveyors of low-intellect heavy metal, a genre which it was alleged had an almost suicidal hold on impressionable American teenage boys. Sure enough, a timely suicide gave a huge media boost to the PMRC cause.

Zappa, whose own lyrics have in the past pulled remarkably few punches, leapt to the defence and argued his case so wittily and articulately on TV, on radio and in the Press that the PMRC promptly cancelled all future debates with him. Zappa summed up the fanatical, almost fascistic views of the PMRC in his cleverly-titled album, *Frank Zappa Meets The Mothers Of Prevention*.

# Ozzy Osbourne

In the entire sphere of rock 'n 'roll, no character exists like John 'Ozzy' Osbourne. At no point along the circumference can anyone of a similarly irresponsible persuasion be found; and to go off at a tangent, never have so many appallingly pithy one-liners emanated from such a mundane music-maker. As a writer/singer/seer Ozzy is outclassed in every single department. As a performer/superstar/presence, however, he sets the agenda.

This is the man who added the final flared vocal to the Black Sabbath harangue, the man who came out of various booze and cocaine binges cackling and demanding more, the man who defecated in a hotel lift and sought to ease the manager's apoplexy by assuring him, 'It's all right, mate. I'm a resident'.

He was born in Aston, Birmingham, in December 1948 and his early career embraced house burglary and slaughterhouse menial work. He took to the abattoir with relish and showed a propensity for separating animals from their heads that was never really to desert him. The burglary was not quite so successful and he spent some time in prison after a botched robbery attempt. Drifting around towards the end of the Sixties he found himself more by accident than design in a local band variously called Rare Breed, Polka Tulk and Earth. The other members, Tony Iommi (guitar), Terry 'Geezer' Butler (bass) and Bill Ward (drums) were similarly disenfranchized young men with a love of basic blues and booze. Eventually the quartet re-named themselves after one of their better songs, Black Sabbath.

Black Sabbath – or The Sabs as most playgrounds in the western world swiftly dubbed them – was an extraordinary concept, almost menacing in its simplicity. Rather than perfect any degree of virtuosity, which was what other self-styled heavy rock bands of the era were doing (Deep Purple, Led Zeppelin), and rather than adhere to a traditional blues outline, as Jethro Tull, Free and Fleetwood Mac were attempting to do, Black Sabbath resorted to brute force. There would be one riff per song, agonizingly intense; there would be wailing lyrics about war, death, paranoia, night and darkness. They were rejected by fourteen record companies. Somehow, however, a record crept out on the Vertigo label and to a chorus of critical scorn the first Sabbath album scaled the charts and became a hit. It would later be commonplace for Black Sabbath to release an album to the immediate and damning reactions of the rock press, but to the manifest delight of the Sabbath army of loyal followers. The appeal of the group was always a mystery to those who could not see it, but irate letters of defence from fans assured the press that the key adjectives were 'strange', 'mystical' and 'eerie' and the key noun 'graveyard'.

The noise of Sabbath on stage was enhanced by the anti-social antics of its lead singer. Singing about madness, he would pretend to be out of his mind. Singing about death and damnation, he would make like he was the Devil. The kids of America, who had gone for Led Zeppelin for their ability to fuse heavy metal and elementary psychological concerns, went customarily ape for Sabbath and pretty soon the new world of drugs, orgies and lakes of alcohol presented itself. When it did, it was not turned away. Osbourne quickly left behind the LSD experiences and moved over to the comfort of cocaine. On their 1972 US tour they did their best to outdo the similarly engaged Zeppelin and Rolling Stones by indulging more for indulgence's sake than any real physical need. Braving the uncertainties of the social disease they entertained floods of groupies and showed liberal gung-ho when offered a new drug thrill. And when the evenings got a bit boring, they would liven them up by setting fire to their drummer, Bill Ward. One time guitarist Tony Iommi poured lighter fuel over Ward's legs and set them alight. Ward needed medical attention.

Strangely enough, this did not lead to Sabbath having to scour the Musicians Available ads for a new drummer. Instead, the rift was between Iommi and Ozzy Osbourne. Iommi was exhibiting a peculiar reluctance to join in the revelry backstage and occasionally admonished Osbourne for his cheerful excess. Osbourne, in retaliation, used to go off stage for a cigarette during Iommi's guitar solos.

Events took a turn for the worse in 1976 when Black Sabbath had their first flop. They had never been a 'singles' band – their only hit single had been 'Paranoid', which they had not attempted to follow up – but they took pride in mammoth album sales. With *Technical Ecstasy*, it was universally decided, they had made a prime bummer. This intrigued the critics, who could not see any difference from previous records, but slagged it off anyway.

Osbourne was now well embedded in cocaine, sick of constant touring and management pressure. One day he snapped and blasted all his farmyard chickens to pieces with a shotgun.

He left Black Sabbath in November 1977 and soon afterwards checked into a mental asylum. By January 1978 he was back in the band, supposedly recuperated. The ensuing album, *Never Say Die*, was arguably the worst of the band's entire career, although it did spawn a hit single (the title track) and thus enabled new legions of Sabbath fans to see their heroes on 'Top Of The Pops'.

The next time, he was sacked. In the summer of 1979 he was replaced by the tiny US singer Ronnie James Dio and, as far as anybody who cared was aware, that was the last we would ever hear from Ozzy Osbourne.

The immediate future was spent consuming as much cocaine and drink as his burly frame could handle. A lifeline was only provided by the intervention of Sharon Arden, daughter of the legendarily terrifying manager/impresario Don, whose Jet Records offered Ozzy a contract.

And sure enough Sharon (to whom Osbourne is now married) was able to sort her charge out well enough for him to audition and hire some backing musicians, two of them well-travelled and hardly adventurous journeymen, the other the exciting American guitarist Randy Rhoads. The band, called Blizzard Of Ozz, made a self-titled album and it was fairly typical stuff, apart from one interesting moment – a song called 'Suicide Solution' – which would haunt Osbourne in later years.

The Ozzy name, it was feared, had been too long out of the public consciousness, so a little publicity was needed. Therefore, a CBS Records convention was chosen as the best place for some Osbourne theatre of

Ozzy Osbourne

the nauseating kind. He was equipped with some white doves, which he produced at the appropriate moment. Then, to the horror of those present, he bit the head off one of them, splattering blood over his trousers, and grinned amiably.

The immediate result was his banishment for all time from the CBS building and the real threat of being thrown off the label. Osbourne now launched himself on an unsuspecting world as the Man Who Eats Whatever You Care To Throw At Him. And so it was that, during a concert of much projectile-lobbing and mirth, Osbourne found himself the recipient of a rubber bat. He raised it to his lips and sank his teeth in . . . oops, not a rubber bat. A real bat.

The joke that circulated at the time was 'Did the bat have to get rabies shots?' Osbourne, of course, did and he did not enjoy the experience. However, a toning-down of his act was not the answer and so mock dwarf-hanging, offal-catapulting and other atrocities took place with regularity whenever the Ozzy Osbourne roadshow came to town.

His biggest mistake, as far as the States was concerned, was to relieve himself in a spot in San Antonio, Texas, without checking out the lie of the land. When confronted by an outraged local, he realized that he had urinated on the Alamo. This defilement of Texans' most sacred heritage got him fined and banned from the district for all time. Soon the Humane Society urged the banning of his shows; meanwhile Osbourne announced his intention to wet the steps of the White House next.

The Osbourne of old has mellowed now – a spell in the Betty Ford Clinic has helped – and aside from the odd hiccup like getting a mouth full of glass when a mirror-shattering trick went wrong during the shooting of a video, his life is almost content. The only major danger came when a young American boy took his life after listening repeatedly to the Osbourne song 'Suicide Solution'. The boy's parents sued him for damages, but the Los Angeles Supreme Court found him not guilty, with the impressive and not totally reassuring quote, 'Ozzy's music may be totally objectionable to many but it can be given First Amendment protection too'.

# Elvis Presley

Make no mistake – if there had never been an Elvis Presley, this book would not exist. Which is not to say that Presley's increasingly odd behaviour leading up to his premature death at the age of only 42 can be entirely explained by the pressure which he felt as the King of Rock, but the expectations of others clearly contributed to his tragic belief that he was infallible, immortal and in a word, Godlike.

When Elvis made his first records for Sam Phillips's Sun label in Memphis, he was a truck driver without prospects, living in a house that was little more than a shack. His father was a convicted criminal who was charged with forgery after altering the figures on a cheque he was given from $4 to $40 in 1937, when Elvis was two years old. This resulted in an initial sentence for Vernon Presley of three years at the infamous Parchman Farm prison (later the title of a celebrated R&B song written by Mose Allison), although Vernon probably served less than one year of his term. Gladys Presley, Elvis's mother, was thus forced to work at menial jobs to earn a pittance in her attempts to provide the necessities for her baby, especially since she actually gave birth to twins when Elvis arrived, although his brother, who was 35 minutes older than Elvis, was stillborn, which made Gladys almost unnaturally protective of her surviving child.

Elvis led a very sheltered life – for many months, his mother took him to school and met him at the school gates afterwards, and he reportedly accompanied her everywhere, which almost certainly embarrassed him as he grew older.

Then came his meteoric and totally deserved rise to fame in the mid-Fifties, when he forged a blueprint for rock 'n' roll from which the world continues to reverberate. The records Presley made before his two years in the US Army between 1958 and 1960 remain the yardstick by which everything which has subsequently occurred in rock 'n' roll is measured. By the time he went into the Forces, he had acquired a manager in the shape of the Macchiavellian self-styled 'Colonel' Tom Parker, previously a carnival hustler who had earned a living in earlier times with his celebrated sideshow featuring dancing chickens – any chicken in a cage whose floor was an electric hotplate would dance, and probably squawk!

Parker shrewdly decided when Elvis's call up papers arrived that any application for deferment might affect his meal ticket's credibility as the archetypal All American Boy, but made sure that enough recordings were available to satisfy public lust for new Elvis material during his stay with Uncle Sam, and even arranged for film footage to be shot in Germany to be used in Presley's fifth feature movie,

*G.I. Blues*, his first film after a two year gap following the release of four commercial blockbusters in under two years prior to his induction as Private US53310761.

The fatal mistake, artistically speaking, was Parker's only partially successful attempt to make Elvis the hillbilly cat into Elvis the all round family entertainer. It became clear that Presley lost control over the material he was told to sing and especially over the movies in which he was obliged to appear, probably because demand for more and more Elvis was insatiable – some years later, an execrable LP of Elvis's between songs dialogue with the dubious title *Having Fun With Elvis On Stage* was released, which contained no singing. To his credit, Elvis was less than keen for this pathetically banal artefact to reach the market, but since by the time of its release, he only had three years to live, and was some distance down the road to self-inflicted oblivion, his protests were over-ruled, as they had been a year earlier, in 1973, when the rights to his back catalogue had been sold by Parker to RCA Records for a reported five and a half million dollars, of which Presley himself only netted $750,000. This must have been one of the shrewdest investments ever made by a record company, as the Presley catalogue continues to sell to the point where the company must have recouped its investment many times over.

At some point, probably around 1970, Elvis seems to have given up worrying about the quality of his output, and may even have begun to despise the fans who, lemming-like, consumed everything marketed with his name on it – dollar bills with his face in the place of that of George Washington have become very popular curios, and it is easy to purchase in gift shops in America facsimiles of Elvis's last will and testament. His marriage to the exceptionally photogenic Priscilla Beaulieu (who later appeared in a leading role in the TV soap opera, *Dallas*) ended in divorce apparently because Elvis preferred the company of the 'Memphis Mafia', a group of bodyguards and hangers-on, many of whom were reportedly prone to agreeing with Elvis, however outlandish and unreasonable his behaviour became. Accusations have been made suggesting that such people's spinelessness strongly contributed to Presley's downfall, and it is hard to deny that a rather more strong-minded approach might have prevented his self-destruct mechanisms from extracting the ultimate toll. On the other hand, he was so convinced, rather like a religious zealot, that everything he thought and did was beyond reproach that he would simply have fired anyone who dared to suggest that he might be human. Then there's the possibly apocryphal story about Elvis playing scrabble – to ensure that he had a better chance of winning, other players were restricted to five tiles (or letters) from which to construct words, while Elvis alone was allowed seven.

His drug intake, perhaps resulting from extreme hypochondria, was said to be immense, and eventually was a major contributory factor to his death on 16 August 1977, when his heart finally gave up the unequal struggle against the weight of increasingly powerful chemicals which were, as far as can be ascertained, prescribed for him by three doctors who were prone to writing out prescriptions if Elvis asked them to. Once again, had any of these medics been sufficently intrepid, Presley's life might have been extended, but, as in the case of the Memphis Mafia, to kill the goose which laid the golden egg would have resulted in banishment from the kingdom of plenty – Elvis was extremely generous with gifts to his close associates – and almost definitely someone else would have emerged who would be prepared to do precisely what Elvis wanted.

The subject of Presley ranks with that of The Beatles as the one about which most books have been written in the annals of rock music, simply because his popularity and influence have never been surpassed. In the world of the cinema, the equivalent figure was Marilyn Monroe, and it is no accident that the legends of Monroe, The Beatles and Presley continue to make headlines decades after the deaths of Elvis, Marilyn and John Lennon – each of the three lived a life which was subject to microscopic scrutiny from the media. Only an extra-terrestrial might be able to survive such pressure, and Elvis Presley, sadly, was a mere mortal.

# Jailhouse Rock

## Dave Crosby

Crosby was the harmonizer, the pure descant that graced records by The Byrds, Crosby Stills And Nash, and Crosby, Stills, Nash And Young. He made one solo LP and he had a few problems.

He started off as a juvenile delinquent in Hollywood. Born in 1941, he was to be expelled from every single school he attended. He drifted into a life of cat burglary, quitting only when he met one of his aged victims. Irresponsibility became his way of life – if he got a girl pregnant, he disappeared for a while.

In the early Sixties he met and joined The Byrds, a California folk group consisting of Jim McGuinn, guitar, Chris Hillman, bass, Mike Clarke, drums, and Gene Clark, vocals. Crosby played rhythm guitar and sang those sweet harmonies.

Thanks to a radical re-working of Bob Dylan's 'Mr Tambourine Man' The Byrds scored a huge success in 1965, a feat they repeated with 'Turn! Turn! Turn!' the same year. As the harmonies got more adventurous and

the songwriting more ambitious, Crosby took to stardom like the

proverbial fish. He would stroll down the boulevard in his green suede cape, sing the praises of LSD to anyone he met (probably in complex scat-jazz form), and he annoyed the hell out of the other Byrds, in particular the pragmatic, mathematical McGuinn.

Crosby was the king of The Byrds' songwriting team, and his songs invariably explored relationships and reflected on the universe in lyrical form.

His rebelliousness made 1967 unpleasant. Sporting his now famous Yosemite Sam moustache, and usually a Cossack hat, he would fraternize with other Californian groups, often comparing them unfavourably with The Byrds. It all reached a head when, at the Monterey Festival in June, Crosby

Dave Crosby, Steven Stills and Graham Nash

played a set with Buffalo Springfield. Then, when he took the stage with The Byrds, he launched into a rap denouncing the Warren Report (on the killing of John F. Kennedy) as a whitewash, and yet again announced how chuffed he was to be able to take lots and lots of LSD. McGuinn was livid. Crosby would last only another few months with the group.

Part of the problem was that Gene Clark had left the group, and although they weren't particularly missing his songwriting contributions (this was at the time of *Younger Than Yesterday*, a masterful album) they did miss his presence. There was now a vacancy for leader, and Crosby was making a very lengthy, very vociferous application.

Another problem was that McGuinn had found religion and changed his name. Crosby, a free-living individual who was not averse to wandering the highways and by-ways of the world in the nude, was writing songs that reflected these practices, and one such song appalled McGuinn. Called 'Triad', it proposed a ménage à trois between people who cannot decide which two ought to pair off. It was rejected instantly by The Byrds and was later recorded by Jefferson Airplane on the *Crown Of Creation* album.

There then came one of the most dramatic firings in the history of rock music. Crosby was sitting at home, no doubt getting into the exquisite LSD mode, when two Porsches screeched up outside. McGuinn was in one, Chris

Hillman in the other. They jumped out, strode into Crosby's living room and really laid it on the line. 'You can't sing,' they told him. 'You can't sing, you can't play and you certainly can't write. Furthermore you are an asshole of the first order and your services are no longer required.' They were met with a shrug. He had other plans anyway.

He bought a yacht with his redundancy money.

His next move was to form a three-winged supergroup with Graham Nash of The Hollies and Stephen Stills of Buffalo Springfield. CSN would prove to be one of the more substantial romantic dreams of the late Sixties.

But then tragedy struck Crosby in September 1969. His girlfriend, Christine Hinton, was killed in a car crash after a cat she was taking to the vet sank its claws into her arm, causing her to swerve into the path of an oncoming bus. Crosby had to identify the body himself.

The Seventies were drug-crazed and inconsequential for Crosby. A bad cocaine habit and a drink problem alienated him from the Stills–Nash axis.

In 1981 he was ambushed by his friends and led to a rehabilitation clinic. He lasted a couple of days. His cocaine intake was so advanced that he was freebasing to get the purest of hits. This is a practice that has seen off a few performers, notably John Belushi, the gargantuan comic. Crosby was indignant – he *wanted* to get high, and was in no way ashamed of being stoned. It wasn't messing with his singing, yet, and he was so persuasive in defence of his addiction that he was allowed to get on with it.

But in the autumn of 1981 he became frail and unreliable, able to sing only for a few minutes at a time and even then in a hoarse whisper.

1982 saw it all go down, and Crosby got himself arrested. Travelling down the San Diego Freeway, he fell asleep at the wheel and made the acquaintance of the central partition. The police turned up, searched the car and found a pistol, some cocaine, a butane torch and a pipe used for freebasing. He explained the gun by reminding the police of John Lennon's assassin – 'If that guy had come after me he'd have been a piece of fucking Swiss cheese,' he said colourfully.

Crosby was believed about the gun, but he was put on three years' probation for the other offences, and ordered to enter a drug rehabilitation programme.

The following month his dressing room was busted at a show in Dallas and police found another gun, more cocaine, and the same freebasing equipment. He was arrested again, and released on bail.

His third arrest came in September, on a charge of assault. Two women were claiming that Crosby had beaten them up. This was later changed to a charge of disturbing the peace, but Crosby had to spend a night in jail when nobody could come up with the $100,000 bail.

Crosby, Stills And Nash's 1983

album, *Allies*, was made almost entirely without Crosby, as the hapless singer retreated into his own glum world.

The Dallas charges came to court in June 1983. He was in a mess, dressing strangely and quite obviously falling asleep on a few occasions. He was found guilty on the drugs charges and the weapons charges, and for a while was looking at 30 years inside. However, sentencing was deferred for a month so that he could tour Europe with Stills and Nash.

It was August when David Crosby turned up at a Dallas courtroom to hear that he had been sentenced to five years' imprisonment for his crimes. A newspaper article on the man shortly afterwards described the life of this 'casualty of cocaine'. All the cars were gone, all the paintings, all the glitter. There remained a butane torch, and a weird-looking pipe.

Unbelievably, it got worse. In December 1985, he was sent to prison again after being arrested for possessing drugs and a gun. This time the clean-up was imperative. He had appeared with Nash and Stills at Live Aid earlier in the year, although Neil Young was expressing reservations about touring with such a bad example to the nation's youth.

In 1988, a revived Crosby teamed up again with his three colleagues on an album called *American Dream*. On a track called 'Compass' he described his lost years thus: 'I have wasted ten years in a blindfold', but assured us that 'like a compass seeking north there lives in me a still sure spirit part.'

81

# Chuck Berry

It's been the fate of many poor wretches in the music business to have hits with the one song in their repertoire which embarrasses them the most. Jeff Beck, for example, must rue the day he ever agreed to saunter his way through 'Hi Ho Silver Lining'. And David Bowie's 1967 'The Laughing Gnome', must have caused the thin white one some fearful ribbing when his callous record company re-released it in 1973. And one might wonder how Paul McCartney sleeps with the fact that his version of 'Mary Had A Little Lamb' is one of his bigger hits.

However, one man who is known to be delighted with the success of a song that appalled just about everyone else is Chuck Berry. Berry's salacious sing-song 'My Ding A Ling', ostensibly a song about the male sexual organ that becomes more inane the closer one analyses it, was one of 1972's raves of the year. It gave Berry his only UK number one hit.

This cruel touch would embitter many performers. After all, Chuck Berry was the man who wrote 'School Days', 'Rock And Roll Music', 'Sweet Little Sixteen' and 'Johnny B. Goode' to name but four. Not all of those songs had even made it to the charts in Britain. To add to his possible misery, he had had to sit back in jail while a succession of inferior talents from both sides of the Atlantic got rich on his formula. *Surely* he would be

livid that, when the great British public saw fit to recognize the genius of one of rock 'n' roll's *creators*, they did so with one of the decade's most annoying songs!

Not a bit of it. Berry is currently somewhere between seventh and eighth heaven, having negotiated clouds nine and ten, and all because the success of 'My Ding A Ling' brought in huge wads of lucre. It is as one of the meanest men in the whole business that a new generation of rock fans are hailing Chuck Berry.

When Charles Edward Berry (born 1926 in St Louis, Missouri) considered career applications in his teenage heyday, it was to the world of hairdressing that he turned. Fortunately for the rest of us he jettisoned the comb and the scissors in favour of a guitar and an amplifier. In 1955 he had his first hit with a song he had written called 'Maybellene', and thereby hangs a tale. Ignorance of record company sharp practice resulted in Berry not studying the small print, and he was horrified to learn that he had only been given a co-credit on the label. He had written the song himself, but a three-way deal was done behind his back. Two people, one of whom he had never even met, were now entitled between them to 66 per cent of his money. Chuck Berry was never ripped off again.

That incident, and repeated incidents of racism directed at Berry, hardened him into a shrewd businessman. The whites in the deep South did not like him at all because he was not the type to be in any way modest about his talent, and also because the white girls showed a tendency to be attracted to this brown-eyed handsome minstrel. Both Berry characteristics antagonized the somewhat less opulent, less confident and presumably less handsome habitués of the whites-only bars.

His songs were, if not exactly sexually explicit, certainly sexually aware. He might have been singing about cars and school and rock 'n' roll music for much of the time, but there was little doubt about why he was so chuffed about 'sweet little sixteen' reaching the age of consent. Brash, brave and brilliant, he tore up the late Fifties with a series of anthems which are still staple fare for all budding rock guitarists. He also had a hand in inventing The Beatles and The Rolling Stones. Without Chuck Berry – no Keith Richards.

In late 1959 Berry was arrested and charged with transportation of a woman across state lines for immoral purposes, under the Mann Act. He had served three years in reform school for robbery and had only escaped a jail term by the skin of his teeth for trying to make it with a sheriff's daughter in Mississippi. The trial for the Mann Act charge was doomed from the moment the judge referred to 'what's his name, this Negro'. Berry's defence was poor and unconvincing, but fortunately the racism of the judge got so prejudicial that he was relieved from duty and a mistrial was announced. At the second trial Berry was found guilty as charged, and sent to prison for three years in 1962. The girl later confessed to being a prostitute.

Berry served sixteen months of the sentence and, on his release in 1964, found that the musical climate had changed. He had some more hits, probably with songs he had written before the prison term, but mostly he concentrated on business interests, setting up an amusement park complex in Missouri called Berry Park.

When he did play, it was noticeable that the famous twinkle in the eye had all but gone, to be replaced by a bitterly realistic level gaze. He did not even have a band. What would happen was that he would turn up at a particular venue and play with a pick-up band. He wouldn't ask their names, they wouldn't know in advance what they were supposed to play, and if they were any good he would pay them. There was a strong element of 'take the money and don't look round till you're in the car and moving'.

The Seventies were a bust time for him musically. Significantly, unlike Little Richard and Jerry Lee Lewis who sometimes found it hard to whip up the same hysteria as they did in the Fifties, Berry has never seemed like becoming obsolete. He toured Britain to great acclaim, although interviewers were taken aback when he denied ever going to prison and said that he had never heard of The Rolling Stones.

A second prison term tainted the Seventies, when the IRS caught up with him. He had under-declared his huge earnings for 1973 by a cool $200,000. Faced with the alternative of a hefty fine or 100 days in the slammer, Berry showed a glimpse of his character when he elected for the latter. Not many people who have served time are enthusiastic about going back, and the decision of Berry to do just that shows what money means to him.

Every now and then a fresh rumour about the man's stinginess crops up. On his last promotional visit to England, in the wake of his film and autobiography, he amazed reporters by only granting them five minutes – or sometimes three – with the tape recorder on, and a further five with the tape recorder off. In order that they did not glean too much free information he pretended to be hard of hearing so that they only managed to ask three or four questions in the time allowed. A TV appearance on a well-known chat show was handled with almost breathtaking contempt by Berry, to the extent that he charged them according to what song they wanted, and would not go on until paid in cash. Keith Richards' involvement in the Berry tribute film could be the most unexpected display of heroism in movie history . . . considering that on a previous occasion Berry had punched Richards in the mouth.

Dark Side of the
LOON

Michael Jackson

# Michael Jackson

If all the peripherals had to be stripped away and all the detritus jettisoned to make way for just one surviving pop star, it would have to be Michael Jackson. This baby-faced, possibly artificially-coloured and allegedly female-hormoned young 30-year-old Peter Pan with Fred Astaire leanings, this snake-fondling llama-loving chimp-championing Howard Hughes manqué is quite simply the biggest phenomenon to hit music since Salieri's death-bed confessions. As if to prove the point he has acquired the rights to most of The Beatles' songs, with reports that he will do an album of cover versions. Paul McCartney, whom he outbidded, is less than chuffed but is momentarily powerless – Jackson's wish is as close to a Papal Bull as makes no difference.

He has made three albums in ten years – *Off The Wall*, *Thriller* and *Bad*. The second of those, released in 1982, is the biggest-selling album of all time. Between them they have spawned fifteen hit singles.

And it is not as though stardom is a new problem for him to cope with. He was a smash hit at five years old, touring with his elder brothers. This singing group, eventually to be named The Jackson Five, may have made him a wealthy young man and an undeniable star, but it also deprived him of a childhood, something he appears to be rectifying these days.

The Jackson Five's first single, 'I Want You Back', released in 1970 on a publicity tidal wave which claimed that the boys had been discovered in Gary, Indiana, by Diana Ross, went to number one in America. From that moment on, every move Jackson made was closely studied. While lesser beacons such as Donny Osmond and David Cassidy – and their respective families – faded from public view to do some much-needed reappraising of life, talent, the universe, etc., Jackson had no time to think.

From the embrace of The Jackson Five he went, with minimal voice-break, to The Jacksons (the same family, but minus Jermaine and plus Randy) and continued the hit-making operation. Separated from the artistic umbilical cord of Tamla Motown and the extremely paternal influence of Berry Gordy Jr, Jackson was able to make his own career decisions and he elected to go for smooth disco soul on his first major solo album *Off The Wall* in 1979. The album was a huge success, as were the unprecedented amount of singles culled from it, but so far as anyone knew, Michael Jackson, just turned 21, was still the lead singer and desperately shy focal point for The Jacksons. This was underlined when a Jacksons album, *Triumph*, came out to great acclaim in 1980. However, any remaining doubt about Michael Jackson's future role in his brothers' group, or for that matter in society, evaporated in 1982 with the release of *Thriller*.

*Thriller* trounced *Off The Wall* in sales in a matter of weeks and its first single, the controversial 'Billie Jean', was to be one of Jackson's finest hours. It was ostensibly a firm denial of a paternity suit – Jackson has claimed to be a virgin – but its intensity and its repetitive hook made it just another accessible pop song, and it duly scored. 'Beat It', featuring heavy metal guitar histrionics courtesy of Eddie Van Halen, followed close behind.

It was at this point that the tabloids began to take more than a friendly interest. It was well known that Jackson was reticent, even mute, when confronted with the Press. But some of his reported behaviour seemed too strange to explain away. Like, for instance, his menagerie in which he kept such prize exhibits as his pet snake Muscles and his pet llama Louie. Like his much-publicized nose job, dramatized in before-and-after shots in newspapers the world over. Like his Peter Pan existence of asceticism and sobriety. Like his courting of older women – Diana Ross, Elizabeth Taylor, even Katharine Hepburn – and the doomed relationship he had with the young actress Brooke Shields.

During the years 1984 and 1985 the myth became a legend. The early months of 1984 saw him severely burned when an advertisement he was making for Pepsi-Cola (he doesn't drink it) ended in disaster. His hair caught fire and he suffered second

degree burns. A month later he cleaned up at the Grammy awards with *Thriller*. He had wept with disbelief when *Off The Wall* only received one Grammy. By March 1984 *Thriller* was the biggest-selling album of all time, its 30 million copies sold representing over 10 per cent of CBS Records' entire income during that period.

That same year he toured with his brothers on the *Victory* Tour (named after a particularly unimpressive Jacksons album) and was the indirect subject of much wrath when the exorbitant ticket prices were announced. There had been ill feeling before this – Michael was believed not to want to tour, while his brothers, angry at being overshadowed, only agreed to his being there for financial reasons. But when the ticket proviso of $28 per ticket and a maximum of four per person came to light, the flak was thrown at Michael Jackson – was he seriously worth this much? After all, Bruce Springsteen had recently toured, selling tickets half as expensive and playing for twice as long. At a press conference Jackson said he would give his share of the takings to charity. His brothers didn't.

In March 1985 his peculiar – some said suspicious – features were being duplicated for inclusion in Madame Tussaud's in London. He came to visit his replica and was the subject of much rumour – was he really bathing in £8,000 worth of Perrier water and had he really insisted on going door-to-door for the Jehovah's Witnesses in West London? – and succeeded in blocking the approach road off with anxious fans eager to catch a glimpse.

In August, while Paul McCartney and Yoko Ono were considering a bid for the rights to old Beatles songs, Jackson nipped in and snapped up the ATV Music catalogue for a mere $40 million. This included the rights to some 5,000 songs, a hefty proportion of which were Lennon–McCartney songs. McCartney, who had collaborated with Jackson on trite but likeable tunes 'Say Say Say' and 'The Girl Is Mine', was known to be miffed, especially when stray Beatles tunes cropped up on US television advertising various products.

In September 1986 it came to light that Jackson was sleeping in a pressurized oxygen chamber. He claimed that this chamber, which had set him back £90,000, would enable him to live until he was 150. In addition he took to wearing surgical face masks on the rare occasions he ventured out into the street. And the greatest furore of all, the one his management swear is complete garbage, was that Jackson was altering his skin pigmentation, that he was actually trying to become a white man. Why? To maximize his appeal? Because he did not like being black? It all seems very unlikely.

What he did try to do, in June 1987, was to buy the remains of John Merrick, the 'Elephant Man' of Victorian times, whose tragic outcast life he believed to be similar in many ways to his own. He offered the London Medical College $1 million for the bones of Merrick, who had died in 1900. The spokesman for the LMC said that any sale would be 'morally wrong'.

# Syd Barrett

The dread rock dinosaur yawns, struggles to its paws and groans. Time to lose another few pounds. Time to say au revoir to the family. Time to tune up that battered old guitar. Time to tour.

Pinkus Floydus – Latin for someone or something that has far outlived its usefulness – is a comparatively young dinosaur. It's only been around since 1965, and even then it spent the first two years hiding underground, perfecting its act. But it seems like forever. That album they made in 1973, *The Dark Side Of The Moon*, a study not so much of madness as of designer boredom, has been in the American charts ever since. Its successor, a smug diagnosis of the music scene entitled *Wish You Were Here*, qualified for a gold disc before it was even released – advance orders saw to that.

And it's been a case of irate teachers, diving bombers and recalcitrant pigs where their live show has touched down. The compact disc generation bows down in humble deference to the glory of the Floyd, for this band is just as fat, just as disillusioned and, ultimately, just as useless as they are.

'Twas not ever thus. When the Pink Floyd started there was a very real case for calling them the most interesting group in the world at the time. Their songs were disarmingly innocent childhood tales, set to some of the most compulsive electronic backing heard in the Sixties. All of this – the name, the songs, the singing, the guitars – came from the strange and suspect mind of Syd Barrett.

Roger Keith Barrett was born in Cambridge in 1946. By all accounts he was an exuberant and intelligent young man, a fast sprinter who simply wanted to get on and do things, without worrying too much about what anyone else thought, or about where it would lead to. Showing early talent at painting, he won a scholarship to Camberwell Art School in London, at the time a hive of activity for artistic teenagers with more than a passing interest in matters spiritual.

But 'Syd' as he was nicknamed was more of a creative brain than most of his contemporaries at art school, and he started to hang out with students from the architecture course at Regent St. Poly, among them Roger Waters, Nick Mason and Rick Wright, who completed the line-up of Pink Floyd.

In the very early days the Floyd stuck to playing cover versions of old R&B faves such as 'Roadrunner' and 'Louie Louie', although Barrett's unique guitar style and tendency to improvise on a theme until there was simply no place else to go meant that the songs bore little comparison to their vinyl originals. Gradually Barrett started to write his own songs, weird hypnotic nursery rhymes with extraordinary hooks and ultra-melodic choruses. In 1967 the band released their first single, 'Arnold Layne'.

Up to that point they had been something of an underground secret, playing at clubs like UFO and the All Saints church hall in Notting Hill, where 'light and sound workshops' were held. The audience would dutifully turn up, laden with LSD and ready to freak out to the music and roll around in great mountains of jelly. The Floyd would be singing their consciousness music, accompanied by some of the most advanced light shows of the time. Barrett would look like a pixie in his paisley shirt and cropped hair.

'Arnold Layne' catapulted them into a bigger league. In many ways it was atypical of Barrett's songwriting. For a start it was less than three minutes long; it was also an extremely contemporary song, far removed from his love of fairy tales and space stories. 'Arnold Layne' was about a man who obtained sexual gratification from stealing women's underwear from washing lines in and around the Cambridge area. It was banned immediately by the pirate radio station, Radio London.

Its follow-up, 'See Emily Play', was a huge success, reaching the top five and winning the group three appearances on Top Of The Pops. A debut album, *Piper At The Gates Of Dawn*, was a triumph. Syd Barrett was, at the age of 21, one of Britain's most successful songwriters. It was ironic, given what outrageous riches later found their way into the pockets of the mark two Floyd, that one of Barrett's chief worries was what to make of even this amount of sudden fame and wealth. Unable to handle it, he was driven to more and more drug excess.

Barrett, of all the members of the band, was most impressed by acid. A deeply sensitive man and an unapologetic student of the ways of the universe, he found its qualities of sound and space invaluable. Not only was he writing better and better, he was tuning in to some previously unexplored wavelengths. In a world of simplicity and decency and kaleidoscopic dreams, his songs seemed to argue, does it really matter about money, property or grown-ups?

The first real evidence that Barrett was finding it difficult to deal with the real world came at the time of 'See Emily Play'. He invited his close friend David Gilmour (who would later replace him as the Floyd's guitarist) to the recording sessions and said nothing to him all day. For the Top Of The Pops appearances he was almost wilfully uncooperative. In the rebellious manner of his hero John Lennon he dressed in rags and mimed atrociously to the words he had written. On their first American tour Barrett showed signs of being in very deep water.

On Dick Clark's Bandstand Barrett's dislike of miming reached a crisis: he did not bother at all, much to the embarrassment of the band. Then, on a teenage religious show hosted by Fifties legend and budding youth counsellor Pat Boone, Barrett posed a few problems for the wizened crooner by not answering any of his questions. He simply stared long and hard into Boone's eyes, a practice he was to adopt later with disturbing frequency. Clearly Barrett was not having fun on the promotional trail.

Back in Britain, on a multi-artist tour featuring Hendrix and The Move among others, Barrett went to pieces completely. When the tour bus reached a new city he would walk off, usually not making it back in time for their appearance that night. When he did remember about the gig, he would blow it by playing the same chord all evening. On one occasion he let his right hand hang limply over the body of his guitar for the entire set while staring in mute perplexity at the people who had come along and ruined his party.

This impossible situation was at least partly rectified by the addition to the Floyd line-up of second guitarist David Gilmour. The plan was for Gilmour to take care of the live aspect of the band while Barrett wrote the songs.

'By the end of the afternoon,' says Waters, 'I thought I'd convinced him that it was a good idea, and he'd agreed, but it didn't really mean very much because he was liable to change his mind about anything totally within an hour.'

It did not work out. Too much

pressure on Barrett resulted in his formal departure in April 1968. He was to pursue a solo career, with the full help and blessing of the Pink Floyd.

The recording of Barrett's first solo album, *The Madcap Laughs*, was probably one of the greatest trials in the history of rock 'n' roll. It certainly exhausted at least two men – Peter Jenner and Malcolm Jones. Eventually an album of sorts was completed, half of it an acoustic set in which Barrett's mind is seen to be on several different planes all at once. At one stage he is singing an extraordinary number called 'If It's In You'.

'Yes I'm thi-i-i-i-i-i-i-inking . . . ' he starts, hitting a high, hysterical note somewhere up in the ether. 'Look . . . I . . . you know . . . I'll *start again*,' he informs the studio.

'Syd,' suggests someone in the control box, 'why don't you try it without guitar?'

'No, it's just the fact . . . of going through it . . . I mean if you . . . if we could cut . . . hmmm . . . '

He starts again. This time he gets it right and the song bursts into life. The words, however, are unlike any ever heard on a rock record. Is this, as psychiatrist R. D. Laing has said, the voice of an incurable madman?

Colonel with gloves Strauss leeches
He isn't love on Sunday's mail
All the fives crock Henrietta
She's a mean go-getter
Gotta write her a letter.

Musicians who played on the record testify to Barrett's craziness. Drummer Robert Wyatt, who had to deal with some completely unplanned time changes, as well as Barrett's inimitable tendency to drop the last beat of a bar and attach it to one further on, tells of the confusion:

'I thought the sessions were actually rehearsals. We'd say "What key is that in, Syd?" and he'd reply, "Yeah" or, "That's funny".'

Barrett's second album, eponymously titled, was if anything an even stranger affair. His voice sounds permanently on the brink of a huge scream that will never end, and the throwaway nursery rhyme at the end about the tiger eating the elephant seems plain nasty when one considers the manic character of the brain that created it.

An interview Barrett did with *Rolling Stone* in 1971 mixes sinister aphorisms with periods of quite subterranean logic:

'I'm sorry I can't speak very coherently. But you know man I am totally together. I even think I should be. I'm full of dust and guitars.'

The interview starts to get a little sad:

'That's all I wanted to do as a kid. Play a guitar properly and jump around. But too many people got in the way. I can't find anybody [to form a band with]. That's the problem. I don't know where they are. I mean, I've got an idea there must be someone to play with.'

He refuses to talk about the drug that led him to the point of despair. 'There's really nothing to say. Once you're into something . . .'

Barrett was admitted into a mental hospital shortly afterwards.

Throughout the Seventies the rumours bred and multiplied. The most common ones had him strolling down the streets of Cambridge in a dress; threatening people with guns; becoming a monk; becoming a tramp; or – best of all – working as a roadie with Pink Floyd. Attempts to get him back in the studio proved useless. He couldn't even play the guitar any more.

In 1982, after years of searching, two French journalists tracked him down to his mother's house in Cambridge. When he opened the door he was Roger Barrett, a paunchy, balding, peculiar man with an odd glint in his eye as if he was saying, 'I knew this would happen'. The journalists had a hard job convincing him that he used to be the demon Syd.

He *was* looking forward to getting back to London, he told them, but he had to wait for the rail strike to end. It was pointed out to him that the strike had ended weeks ago. 'Oh, thanks very much,' he said, touched. No he didn't play guitar, or paint, just watched TV and waited. For what? Well, he didn't really know. Eventually the voice of his mother was heard calling him and he went inside, looking frightened.

It's a matter of some conjecture whether Barrett was a fragile individual before he discovered LSD. Psychiatrists see recognizable patterns in his condition – the sensitive youth who suddenly goes schizophrenic. LSD, they reckon, merely expedited matters. Whatever, there is little doubt that Roger 'Syd' Barrett was the victim rather than the hero of his own story. In October 1988, in a 'shock horror' story on the musical genre Acid House which was sweeping Britain at the time, the *News Of The World* ran a two-page article on Syd Barrett. Juxtaposing then-and-now photographs to admittedly devastating effect, they featured a photo of the reclusive star in his garden. He looks overweight, balding and unfriendly. Never before had he so resembled his former colleagues in The Pink Floyd.

# Keith Moon

'The production of our records has got nothing to do with sound. It's got to do with trying to keep Keith Moon on his fucking drum stool.' – Pete Townshend, The Who, 1970.

Now and again the mighty Gods of sweet serendipity smile on the beleaguered beacons of tabloid journalism and come up with a character so awesomely dangerous and dedicated to the perpetual pursuit of the offensive, the surreal and the illegal that not even the slightest degree of newshounding is necessary. The stories write themselves, arriving at the office in glorious rounded form, with a beginning, middle and end, none of which are especially believable but all of which conspire in a recipe of prime shock-horror.

Keith Moon was such a character.

Ostensibly the drummer in a rock band, he waged a personal war against the forces of complacency and decency which saw him revered far and wide by his teenage acolytes as the all-time champion of Going A Bit Too Far. And in one of those wonderful instances where the English language proves itself perfectly equipped to deal with its exponents, a concise, witty and irrevocable soubriquet provided itself. From the time he tore the stuffing out of his first hotel pillow until the pitiful anti-climax of his death at 32, Keith Moon was known universally as Moon The Loon.

It is said that the 15-year-old Moon passed his audition for The Who in 1962 by demolishing his drum-kit. Thereafter he embarked on a 16-year orgy of fun and destruction that made him the scourge of hotel managers everywhere and the ultimate party guest. Listed below are a series of his exploits, in no particular order (it could hardly be argued, after all, that Moon *matured*). The authors humbly suggest that these vignettes be read aloud in order to give them their full dramatic impact.

Upon waking one night to a fierce hunger, Moon decides to treat himself to a chicken. Unfortunately the kitchens in his hotel are long since closed and his whim cannot be indulged. None too worried, Moon breaks into the hotel kitchens and raids the fridge, relieving it of its contents. He then repairs to his room, stuffs himself with chickens and finds to his chagrin that there are still some left, which he is too full to eat. There is really only one solution for him. He kicks them around the room until they are in bits, then replaces them in the fridge. Casually flipping a wad of tenners over the reception desk the next morning, he tells the management, 'By the way, this is for those chickens I had last night.'

One year The Who finds itself on a Sixties-style package tour, with Traffic and The Herd making up the numbers. The Herd, who were led by blond dreamboat Peter Frampton (who would later become an American rock 'n' roll icon), had a contemporary hit with a moody piece of nonsense called 'From The Underworld'. Onstage it was The Herd's habit to have a gong lowered behind the drummer for him to hit at the climax of the number. Bored by watching this comical stunt night after night, Moon bribes a stagehand to let him lower the gong at the appropriate moment. Sure enough this moment arrives and Moon carefully lowers the gong from the beams over the stage. The drummer of The Herd gets ready to give it a swipe when suddenly it is snatched out of his reach. The audience is then treated to the spectacle of the drummer leaping up in the air trying to strike his gong, while Keith Moon lifts it further and further out of his reach.

A Who gig in San Francisco is just about ready to start, except that there is one small problem. The drummer is in Los Angeles. Eventually located in a darkened hotel room, he proves impossible to wake. Not only that, but the lights won't come on when the switch is operated. It is a situation easily explained – both Moon and the lights are knackered because he finished off the previous evening's revelry by flinging his colour television at the chandelier.

At that same gig The Who's guitarist Pete Townshend becomes increasingly distressed at the erratic timekeeping of his drumming friend. He's slowing down by the bar, as the night's potion of drink and drugs bubbles in his system. 'Play faster!!'

roars Townshend, 'play *faster*'. Moon is quite obviously in a spot of bother, so a doctor is summoned with the necessary pick-me-ups in his syringes. During a quiet section in the song Moon is given a twin boost in his ankles. He proceeds to play like a madman, flailing away at his cymbals and lashing into his drums. All the time Townshend is screaming, 'Play slower, play *slower*!!'

Driving cars is something Moon never showed a lot of skill in. Opting for the passenger seat for one particular journey, he nevertheless wishes to get involved, to help out the driver. So he elects himself operator of the gear lever. When he feels the car is going fast enough – say 120 mph (190 km/h) – he slams the car into first gear. The car, perfectly understandably, is suddenly in great pain and flees away from the road to find a quiet spot to lick its wounds. It chooses a secluded bank of a reservoir and perches there, trembling ominously.

On another occasion, having collided in a drunken stupor with a meat lorry, he offers to pay the ensuing fine by American Express.

The famous incident, the one in which Moon's Rolls-Royce was driven by its owner into a swimming pool and left to drown, is not strictly factually correct. He does attempt a marriage between several thousand pounds' worth of automobile and a large amount of water, but it's his ornamental pond that ends up having a Rolls-Royce for a guest. He drives it

Keith Moon

there because he says he wants to kill himself, and he does not receive the required amount of outraged protests.

This is a trick he gets up to a lot – one time he leaps off a high windowsill into the sea below. Terrified, as the drummer is in no fit state to swim, the rest of the band commence a search that lasts many hours and involves coastguards, lifesavers and policemen. When Moon is sure that they have called off the search and are phoning around all the available drummers in the area, he emerges grinning. 'Bet you thought I'd never do it.'

The pick-me-up trick does not work at every gig. One time Moon is playing so half-heartedly that even the audience notices it. Despite Townshend's colourful exhortations to the drummer, he clearly can't cut it and eventually he collapses into his drum-kit. Looking a little sheepish The Who carry him off.

Backstage Moon is given oxygen (always kept handy since the very nature of his percussion technique suggests that it will prove indispensable one day) and shows signs of recovery. The rioting in the hall is averted; The Who re-take the stage. One song into the resumption and Moon is face down in his kit again. This time the gig's really over, and Moon is taken away to hospital – partly because he looks half-dead but mostly because everyone's intrigued to find out exactly what he's on. When his stomach is pumped out it turns out that he's been taking the exact same

stuff that is used for tranquillizing gorillas.

More hotel fun ensues when Moon, in a fit of anti-American hysteria, decides to booby-trap the lift. With a waterbed. But the waterbed proves impossible to lift and instead of manoeuvring it out into the hall he succeeds only in tearing it. Inevitably, its contents spill out all over the carpet of his hotel room. Unphased, he commences to swim in the liquid. Then, bored by the proceedings, he rings the management and complains in tones of outraged English righteousness that he has been given a defective waterbed and demands suitable compensation.

Complaints about Moon occur with chilling frequency during his sojourns in the world's hotels. For a man who likes his music loud (his penchant is for surf music, as practised by The Beach Boys and Jan And Dean), the apoplectic plaintiff is never too far away. The manager of one establishment buttonholes him with regard to the sonic boom emanating from his room. 'It's a noise,' he says with distaste, pointing in the general direction of the cacophony. Moon retaliates by blowing up his room with a Cherry Bomb. 'Now *that's* a noise!' he tells the manager.

Wherever The Who stay there tends to be a lot of police. There are more than usual one time when Moon picks the hotel manager's wife to blow up. Surprisingly, hotels in and around the New York area have been strangely reluctant to admit The Who and those that do – the Holiday Inn chain for example – demand a hefty sum up front.

It's the Cherry Bombs that do it. Particularly deadly fireworks, they bring Pete Townshend out in a cold sweat:

'I was in his [Moon's] room and all the paint round the door knocker was black where he had been putting these things in the key-hole. I happened to ask if I could use his bog and he just smiled like this [maniacal grin] and said, "sure". I went in and there was no toilet – just a sort of S bend coming out of the floor! "Christ, what the fuck's happened," I asked. And he said, "Well, this Cherry Bomb was about to go off in my hand, so I threw it down the bog to put it out." "Are they powerful?" I asked, and he nodded. "How many of them have you got?" I said with fear in my eyes. He said, "500", opening up a case which was full to the top with Cherry Bombs.'

One reaches, however, a plateau of destruction – everything levels out. The act of destruction becomes a bit tedious since it's the end result that counts, the sheer joy of admiring your own handiwork. Therefore, Moon starts to cut out some of the violence and concentrate on the end effect. As Townshend puts it, 'he arranges it artistically'. It doesn't sound like havoc, but it sure looks it. Television sets are taken apart, cabinets unscrewed, baths filled with tomato ketchup (occasionally with a plastic leg sticking out), furniture overturned just so.

His practical jokes take on the surreal touch of an inspired clown. Once he hires six girls from a massage parlour and persuades one of them to take part in a ruse. He gets his personal assistant to telephone for help, saying, 'Come quick, Moon's gone mad, he's killed this chambermaid . . . ' When the door is eventually smashed in the scene to greet the intruders is priceless – one of the girls lying with a mouthful of tomato ketchup, her legs splayed all over the place, Moon weeping tears of remorse in the corner, and the rest of the party choking back hysterical laughter.

Airports are another favourite haunt. Equipping himself on one journey with a toy gun, he hides behind a pillar at an airport terminal and waits for someone to come by. He hears footsteps approaching and leaps out screaming threats. He's picked a policeman. Later the same night, having been released from police custody only on the production of a reasonable sum of money, he destroys a computer terminal at the same airport. And it's back to the station, where this time the money's not good enough.

Messing with the authorities becomes a Moon hobby. Convinced – as it happens, correctly – that his cherubic charm and laddish bonhomie will rescue him from any scrape, he decides to hold up a security van. So, having taken care of the first half of the plan, which is to run it off the road, he contemplates the next move. Attack? Well, of course they might have guns.

Sod it, he decides, and drives off. Minutes later he is surrounded by police. It transpires that the van he chose to hassle was carrying a million pounds in used notes. It takes all his crafty expertise to spring himself from the police noose this time.

One time he is not so lucky. Driving away from a gig he is besieged by hysterical fans, whom he prefers to avoid. He speeds up. The point is, he should not even be driving. Quite apart from the fact that he is drunk and does not possess a driving licence, he actually employs a chauffeur to drive for him. Moon thinks the chauffeur has run on ahead to get out of the way of the screaming fans, but he has not. Some youths have kicked him into the path of Moon's speeding car . . .

Not that Moon ever uses cars for their usual purpose. Even when he uses them for transport he adds a twist to the tale. In the mood for a tincture or two, Moon orders his assistant to drive him to a nightclub, through the West End of London. The drummer stretches out on the bonnet. He is not wearing any clothes. The route they take is a fairly well-populated one and people are commencing to point and stare as they arrive at the club. Once in the club (one wonders if he thought it was a 'members only' establishment) he spots Mick Jagger and his wife of the time, Bianca. Merrily he chats away as they consume their meals. Oddly enough, they elect not to stay for coffee.

In most of these incidents he has an accomplice, either someone he has tricked into participation, or someone who is as wrecked as he is. Never a man to use one pill where two will do, he finds himself increasingly unconscious and prostrate amid female company. However, he does have one close friend and rival, the celebrated English eccentric Viv Stanshall. Stanshall's band, The Bonzo Dog Doo Dah Band, occupies a special place in comedic/musical relations thanks to his dark wit and Neil Innes' splendid tunes, and he is as daring and tasteless as Moon himself.

The apex of their high jinks takes place one Saturday when they raid their respective costume wardrobes and come up with a sinister Nazi look. Emerging into bright British daylight they are appalled to learn that practically nobody is shocked by their antics. Bright idea time. Why not go to Golders Green, the heart of the Jewish community? Not only will *they* be appalled by the sight of two high-ranking Nazis sallying forth up the High Street, but it's the Jewish holy day *too*.

Not even the avowed shock tactics of the punk generation phased Keith Moon. Drawing up outside the Marquee Club in his Rolls-Royce one evening, he is met by a hail of abuse. He gets out of his car, furious, slamming doors and looking dangerous. He berates the queue of punks. 'Look at you,' he sneers. 'I've never queued to get into a club in my life!' With that he barges to the head of the queue and disappears into the club. Once inside he finds himself the victim of every brash punk kid with a mate to impress. One youth gives him particular grief. 'You don't mean nothing to me,' he tells Moon, 'nothing means nothing to me.' Moon snatches the boy's drink off him and knocks it back. 'Oy, watcha doing?' howls the aggrieved wretch. 'Well, you said nothing means nothing to you . . .'

Throughout the hectic, dangerous years Moon (it seems astonishing now) kept up a standard of rock drumming that has never been equalled. Behind his ridiculously large kit with its mountains of tom-toms and scores of cymbals, he sweated and grimaced as his extraordinary stickwork spliced through every one of Townshend's riffs. Sometimes he destroyed his kit afterwards. Sometimes he did not need to – it was hanging in bits when he finished playing on it.

Once, during a fit of the blues, he became convinced that he could improve substantially. Hearing that the great jazz drummer Philly Joe Jones was giving lessons in London, Moon trooped along. Jones did not know him from Haile Selassie. 'Beginner or advanced?' he asked. 'Ummm . . . advanced,' shrugged Moon. 'All right, man,' said Jones. 'Show me what you can do.' Moon assumed the position behind the kit and let fly with his customary crazy arm-swinging hysteria, venting years and years of spleen, leaving the kit in a pulsating, shaking heap. Jones gaped at him. 'You make a living doing that?' Moon grinned. 'About 50 grand a week, actually.' 'Get out of here, man,' said Jones, 'I'd only spoil it.'

Moon died, aged 31, in September 1978. He was taking anti-alcoholism tablets at the time. One night he took 32, more than twice the recognized lethal dose.

The Who did not, as Led Zeppelin, later did, call it a day. They hired Kenny Jones, a former member of The Small Faces and in every way the antithesis of Moon, and they made a few more albums. You'll probably find them in the bargain bins at your local record store.

# THE GREATEST ROCK 'N' ROLL $WINDLE$

## Malcolm McLaren, Sid Vicious and The Sex Pistols

In 1976, as people in the know now agree, things had gotten just a little stale. Well, more than just a little. Unless you were a coke fiend you couldn't keep up with the towering crass purveyors of tedious soft rock who kept their real athletics for off the field, and saw rock music as a means to owning their own pharmacy. The records they made were fun-defying exercises in fretboard contemplation. But they were snapped up by the million by spaced-out kids suckered by the handle this nowhere music had been given – progressive rock. Snails progress too, if you think about it. But not too fast.

The revolution was not planned. A chap called Wally Nightingale (a tribute to his importance is that few can recall his surname) had put together a band in school, a good times get-together that gradually got more serious as the musicians learned to play. Two of them were Steve Jones on guitar and Paul Cook on drums.

Wally, after his dad objected to the racket, was ousted. A gentleman called Glen Matlock, a serious musician in comparison with the others, came in on bass.

It was these boys' habit of an afternoon to frequent a Kings Road joint called 'Sex' (Matlock worked there) which doubled as a go-ahead clothes shop and a forum for vacant teenage chat. The proprietor, one Malcolm McLaren, took an interest in the band, advising them on what songs to attempt and turning them on to The New York Dolls, whom he had managed at a particularly traumatic time in their career.

One day, when a search for a suitable lead singer had been turning up nothing, a precariously-dentured youth of speedfreak hue entered the shop, auditioned to the strains of Alice Cooper on the jukebox, and got the gig. Nobody considered for a moment that he could sing, but he had that lunatic *joie de mort* that would make him one of the great rock 'n' roll howlers.

They started to play live, gatecrashing college gigs where they would last maybe three songs if they were lucky, and something about the audience reaction – the mindless violence, the beer wars, the teddy bear terrorism – told them they were on to a good thing. 1976 saw them congeal into a working unit, with real songs, a razor edge and even some

**Sid Vicious**

vestiges of a fan club. One of their followers, a lanky youth named John Simon Ritchie, later to become famous under another name, instigated a new form of dancing. Oppressed on all sides by people just as immobile as he was, he opted for the vertical hold. A major novelty was born; the pogo, the punk movement in pure physical potency, took off.

Another fashion accessory, the safety pin, came into prominence as a patent of the singer. This recent acquisition, a highly-charged and verbal lad named John Lydon, had been re-named Johnny Rotten and he was to affront student audiences and the high hippie count thereof for the next year.

The summer of 1976 saw all sorts of bands spring up in The Sex Pistols' wake. Some were pretty good – The Damned, The Clash – some were rather dreadful – Eater, Slaughter and The Dogs. At a seedy Oxford Street venue, the 100 Club, a festival was held for all to show their colours. The violence of the crowd took a horrible twist when a glass thrown towards the front ricocheted off a pillar and shattered into a girl's eye.

The punk thing was still in the pre-media stage and everyone was bidding for territory. All the small places where the gigs took place – as well as the 100 Club there was the Nashville, Dingwalls and the Marquee – were easy to get to, and difficult to leave once you were inside.

At this point the big guns moved in. Impressed by what they took to be a rowdier, more rabid version of The Rolling Stones, EMI began negotiations with the Pistols. A contract was formally signed in October 1976 and work began on the first single, a confrontational stream of jagged one-liners called 'Anarchy In The UK'.

It was released in November 1976 but weak distribution meant that it lost momentum low in the charts. A tour of Britain was being organized and some cool publicity was needed . . .

After the fuss of the Bill Grundy incident died down nobody was any the wiser: were they plied with alcohol or weren't they? The terse statement from Thames TV pointed out that no-one is allowed so much as a can of lager before 5.30. But there are pubs in and around the Euston area . . .

It was 1 December 1976 and in a stroke of inspired public relations one of the researchers at the 'Today' office booked The Sex Pistols and their friends to appear on the programme and explain to Bill Grundy just exactly what all this nonsense was all about.

They were the last item on the show, gathered in a malevolent giggling semi-circle at Bill Grundy's feet. He laid into them right from the start. He'd heard that punks were non-materialistic chaps, anarchists and so on, and didn't this jar slightly with the news that EMI had spent £40,000 on them? Not at all, answered one of the band. The more the merrier. In fact, the more the merrier the sooner the better, since they'd spent the first lot.

Grundy then started on a totally

different tack, listing some classical composers – Beethoven, Mozart, Bach and Brahms – presumably as a preamble for dismissing the Sex Pistols as musical buffoons. But he got no further. 'They're wonderful people,' chimed in a Pistol. Grundy was confused, lost for a reply. 'Well, suppose they turn other people on?' he floundered. 'That's their tough shit,' muttered Johnny Rotten. Grundy pounced on the expletive. The Pistols started to mock him, one of them suggesting that 'he's like yer Dad, inne, this geezer? Or yer grandad'.

Grundy picked on a waif-like girl at the front. 'I've always wanted to meet you,' she said. Perhaps, he suggested, they could meet afterwards. 'You dirty sod,' castigated a Pistol. And then Grundy lost the rag, altogether, forever, making TV history. Lapsing into the vernacular and desperate to regain control he said, 'Well, keep going, chief. You've got another five seconds. Say something outrageous.' 'You dirty bastard.' More, more. 'You dirty fucker.' Grundy tried sarcasm: 'What a clever boy.' The Pistols volleyed it back: 'What a fucking rotter.'

Grundy was a broken man. In his usually fluent outro-to-camera he realized what he had done and tried to make amends. 'Well, that's it for tonight. The other rocker, Eamonn, I'm saying nothing about him, will be back tomorrow. I'll be seeing you soon. I hope I'm not seeing *you* again (to the Pistols). From me though, goodnight.' The Thames switchboard found

itself in overload mode as the complaints reached saturation level. A Thames TV spokesman apologized on behalf of his beleaguered station and assured shocked viewers that Bill Grundy had been 'carpeted'.

It was, like the Thorpe affair and the Parkinson shenanigans, a glorious opportunity for people who have never transgressed a single law in their lives to go into a quiet studio somewhere and vent spleen. MPs were lobbied, newspapers were contacted, the IBA were notified. Bill Grundy, whose career thus far had been fairly unspectacular, became a Hitleresque villain. He provided the punchline to the affair when he was collared by a *Daily Mail* reporter. 'You'll get nothing from me,' he said, 'so you can fuck off.'

The Grundy wife and kids were dragged out to testify that Grundy senior never swore in front of them and indeed was very opposed to this sort of carry-on, although Mrs Grundy conceded that 'with the boys in the pub' her husband occasionally used 'some pretty strong language'.

The Sex Pistols were now stars. As Grundy was suspended and the ire of Britain aired on every available lively letters page the question of who these people were and what they wanted suddenly posed itself. There were enough defenders of their behaviour and supporters who claimed they had been provoked to keep the story running for a long time. Even arch punk terrorist Bill Haley, the scourge of suburban cinemas everywhere, was pressed for a comment. 'I'm all for entertainment,' answered the big man, 'but I've got a teenage daughter. And I wouldn't like her to listen to some of the language these fellows use.'

From this point on, every time The Sex Pistols drew breath – individually or collectively – the heat was on. The press was out in force at Heathrow Airport to report on a rumpus in the VIP lounge.

They allegedly saw Pistols vomiting in corridors, spitting at other passengers and at each other, and concluded that the KLM officials gave them a VIP send-off because the other passengers on the Amsterdam flight refused to travel with them. One such plaintiff moaned, 'I think they must have been drinking and they looked as if they needed a good wash.'

The result was that EMI sacked them. Appalled by the extent of the bad publicity, and reasoning that the sale of The Sex Pistols on a worldwide basis would be a hazardous enterprise, the gentlemen of Britain's most prestigious record company baulked at the future. For one thing, there was Jubilee Year coming up, and the group had written a song that went, 'God save the Queen/Her fascist regime'.

Malcolm McLaren was rumoured to have taken EMI for £50,000 – £10,000 more than Grundy had accused them of getting. The record company's statement, while stating that a lot of the press reports had been greatly exaggerated, said that EMI felt unable to promote the group's records internationally in view of the adverse publicity.

Early 1977 saw bassist Glen Matlock sacked, allegedly 'for liking The Beatles'. Matlock made no secret of his musicianship and the fact that he was keen for the Pistols to develop as a first-rate rock 'n' roll band. His dislike of Rotten's lyrics and his irritation at the unprofessional attitude of the singer (like when Rotten threatened to beat him up onstage for example) distanced him from the rest of the Pistols. He was replaced by an associate of Rotten's, one-time fan of the band and instigator of the pogo: John Simon Ritchie. Taking the *nom de guerre* Sid Vicious, he decided he could learn how to play the bass.

It was some comment on how McLaren saw the Pistols developing that he replaced their best musician with someone who could not even play. But Sid was an image man par excellence, a dead-end walking spike, with a chronic heroin problem and a love of beating up people smaller than himself.

On 9 March The Sex Pistols signed with A&M Records for £25,000.

On 16 March The Sex Pistols left A&M Records for £50,000.

The legend was now hysterical and cash-laden. The great rock 'n' roll swindle had taken place. A&M, it seems, had been persuaded that The Sex Pistols could be controlled, that they were merely of the order of boisterous boys, and the signing took place outside Buckingham Palace. Then came an incident in which the band were alleged to have visited their new record company to say hello and vomited all over the carpets. The staff, in a state of shock, protested, trusty A&M artist Rick Wakeman protested, and the deal was rescinded (with, of course, compensation being paid to the artists).

In May 1977 they signed with Virgin. Their second single, 'God Save The Queen', was released the same month. With newspaper outrage in Jubilee year, radio bans, and a particularly uninspiring Rod Stewart single, it failed to reach the coveted number one spot in the charts. But there seems little doubt that it was the fastest selling record of the year. In June, Virgin hired a boat and sailed a party down the Thames. Eleven people, including McLaren, were arrested on its return. The backlash had started; it would not be long before the Great British Public joined in.

In one week in June there were three savage attacks on Sex Pistols. The first incident was an assault on their art director Jamie Reid, who had a leg broken and his face smashed up. Incident number two gave Johnny Rotten a slashed face in a brutal razor attack by men who felt that the Queen was getting too hard a time from these characters, and perhaps someone ought to stick up for her. In the third attack, drummer Paul Cook was set upon by five men outside Shepherd's Bush tube station. He was stabbed several times and bludgeoned on the back of the head with an iron bar. The press expressed a wish to take photographs of the scars.

Nobody said it would be easy, but democracy's a funny old game, as The Sex Pistols found out when they released their debut LP, *Never Mind The Bollocks, Here's The Sex Pistols*. Titled after a catchphrase coined by guitarist Steve Jones, it zoomed straight to number one in the album charts and led to a dilemma for retailers up and down the country – should they promote it in their windows, or hide its lurid cover in a brown paper bag, or what? Should they stock it at all? The law decided for them when a test case was brought against a Nottingham retailer, charging him with a contravention of the Indecent Advertisements Act (1889). The three magistrates found him not guilty, although they could not resist further comment: 'Much as my colleagues and I wholeheartedly deplore the vulgar exploitation of the worst instincts of human nature for the purposes of commercial profits, we must reluctantly find you not guilty.'

A newspaper article the same month, December, lambasted the group over the title of one of their new songs, 'Belsen Was A Gas'. A spokesman from the Board Of Deputies Of British Jews expressed his shock and disgust over the song, which the band had been playing on their tour of Holland: 'I can only say that theirs is a very degenerate art if they can compose songs like this with such offensive titles.'

In 1978 The Sex Pistols went on an

ill-advised tour of the American South, during which all the chickens in the coop came home to roost and combustion occurred. Reports filtered through to the British papers of sporadic outbreaks of violence directed at the band, and of Sid Vicious's extraordinary behaviour on stage. At one show in Memphis he stabbed himself with a knife. The wound was dressed but he pulled the dressing off later in the show to expose the bloody gash.

Rotten got bored and headed off to New York. Vicious was admitted to hospital after a drug overdose, and the two urchin rockers, Jones and Cook, sallied off to Rio to hang out with Great Train Robber and hero of both, Ronnie Biggs. This last trio, the least likely bunch of musicians, actually continued as The Sex Pistols throughout the summer, releasing a Biggsian epic variously titled 'No-One Is Innocent' and 'Cosh The Driver' which boasted the lyrics, 'God save Martin Borman and Nazis on the run'. Johnny Rotten, when asked, claimed that The Sex Pistols had ceased operations when he left.

In October 1978 the dead body of Sid Vicious's girlfriend, Nancy Spungen, was discovered at New York's Chelsea Hotel. Vicious, who claimed not to be able to remember any of the previous evening's events, was arrested and charged with her murder. She had been stabbed repeatedly with a knife.

Five days later he was released on bail of $50,000, but he was a hopeless case by now and was back on remand in a matter of weeks, after beating up Patti Smith's brother Todd in a nightclub. In February he was released on bail again, for the same amount, and a day later he was dead. He died from heroin which his mother later claimed to have provided.

Malcolm McLaren kept the scam going a little while longer, until the film *The Great Rock 'n' Roll Swindle* was completed. There were also assorted compilation LPs with titles like *Carri On Sex Pistols* and *Flogging A Dead Horse*. By then Jones and Cook were generally unemployed, Rotten had reverted to his real name John Lydon and was fronting an arty combo called Public Image Limited, steadfastly refusing to play Pistols songs, and McLaren was tampering with the image of one Adam Ant.

When McLaren next burst on the scene, in the early Eighties, it was with a band called Bow Wow Wow. They were fronted by a 15-year-old singer called Annabella Lwin whom McLaren had reportedly rescued from a launderette. He recreated Manet's 'Dejeuner sur l'Herbe' with Annabella naked for the cover of the band's debut album. McLaren planned to branch out into child porn and drew up a blueprint for an underage sex magazine called *Chicken*. EMI dropped the band and McLaren picked up another cool £55,000. When last seen he was making an album combining rock and opera called *Madame Butterfly*. It is highly likely that we will be hearing more from him.

# The Beastie Boys

The year and a half of explosive notoriety that Malcolm McLaren succeeded in wheedling out of The Sex Pistols seemed a paltry deal at the time. Considering that – at least while they had Glen Matlock on bass – they were a fantastic rock 'n' roll band, they deserved better than the usual grim teenybopper spread.

The Beastie Boys were famous for approximately three months.

From March to May 1987 The Beasties, as the tabloid scribes swiftly dubbed them, preached a barely coherent gospel of complete mayhem, drunkenness, misogyny, irresponsibility, teenage rebellion and indolence. They sought, and found, religion in a can of Budweiser.

With only one hit single under their belts they were being hailed as (depending on which way you vote) the most exciting sunsplash to hit rock 'n' roll's tired terrain in years, or the single most depressing cloud on the entire horizon. In time-honoured tradition, questions were eventually asked in the House Of Commons and, no, they could not decide either.

The Beastie Boys were, as the media went to great pains to inform us, three affluent brats from New York in their early 20s. Their names were Adam Horowitz, Adam Yauch and Michael Diamond, although they preferred to do business under the clipped soubriquets AdRock, MCA, and Mike D, respectively. The streetwise nomenclature fooled no one. Horowitz was the son of noted playwright Israel Horowitz and Yauch senior was a successful architect.

They swooped into a musical context with the advent in New York of rap music. Rap was an almost exclusively black sound and rap artists such as Run DMC and LL Cool J are highly respected, not only as first class vinyl merchants but also as social commentators on working-class black issues, things that affect the everyday humdrum of the street-hogging neighbourhood kids. Well, The Beastie Boys ran on similar rails. They too sang about what was important to them. And thus it was that in March 1987 the British charts were infiltrated by a song called '(You Gotta) Fight For Your Right (To Party)'. The song was a screaming lament of soiled teen angst along lines that dumb kids everywhere can identify with. Kids wanna party, Mom says no, kids hate Mom, life's not fair, etc.

The video for this event was a Mack Sennett tribute and a half. The custard pie war that spoke volumes about the trio's basically childish harmlessness was deemed unsuitable for airing by the BBC. The song was a hit anyway and the image of the three as uncouth, cursorily-washed beer-swillers and porno-connoisseurs – lager louts before the genre received its tag – stuck fast. There was something vaguely heroic, perhaps even godlike, about three well-educated youths who simply wanted to get as drunk as possible as quickly as possible and then wreak maximum havoc on the local squares.

Another single, 'No Sleep 'Til Brooklyn', and the album from which both songs came, *Licensed To Ill*, were eagerly added to the collection. *Licensed To Ill*, which had horrified the upper echelons at CBS Records (especially when the Beastie Boys announced their intention to call it 'Don't Be A Faggot') now embarrassed them with its success, and the boys made a rapid mutation from sewer rats to personae gratae. The door was open to them everywhere they went . . . although the truly cautious took it off its hinges as a safety measure.

In interviews The Beastie Boys kept up the pace. Rather than capitulate into admissions of hype and gimmickery they acted just like they were supposed to, and indulged in tasteless memories that showed a sense of humour more off the wall than old Humpty himself. Mike D claimed to have been born without any legs. He had originally intended to introduce the concept of 'handicap rap'. Then a miracle presented itself and he awoke one morn to discover the necessary limbs in full working order. AdRock went one better (or worse). He told of how he had shaved all his hair off at school and claimed to have had chemotherapy. This was a painfully ironic touch given what would happen in a matter of months . . .

When a tour was announced for May 1987 there was a certain amount of consternation, to say nothing of fear. Peter Bruinvels was not the only MP to wonder aloud if Great Britain, what with one thing and another, really *needed* these chaps. He suggested a ban by the Home Secretary on the grounds that they were obscene and depraved. He forgot to call them 'obnoxious', their favourite word.

The joke was that The Beastie Boys had already been to Britain to play the previous year, and there had been absolutely no trouble at all. In fact the only notably notorious highlight of 1986 was Michael Jackson's refusal to let them record The Beatles' 'I'm Down' (Jackson owns the rights to The Beatles' back catalogue).

The horror of what Britain could be letting itself in for was spelled out in huge letters by Gill Pringle of the *Daily Mirror* pop gossip column in May.

The Beastie Boys had been invited to participate at the Montreux Festival, a multi-media event where top stars of the day mime to their songs and everyone pretends not to notice. The rumour had it that their invitation was a deliberate carte blanche to cause trouble, and liven up an increasingly uninspiring festival.

While they were in Montreux they were asked to sign autographs for some terminally ill children. These kids had been brought to the festival by the Dreams Come True charity, and they were fans of The Beastie Boys.

The following day the *Mirror*, under the screaming headline 'Pop Idols Sneer At Dying Kids – Shame Of

Rampaging Stars', printed allegations that The Beastie Boys had responded to the children's request with the words, 'Go away, you fucking cripples', and had laughed at the 'baldies'. The allegation was immediately denounced by The Beastie Boys and by the Dreams Come True representative as a complete fabrication. Gill Pringle, who wrote it, stuck to her guns.

The aftermath was reminiscent of the Sex Pistols/Bill Grundy incident. A DJ on London's Capital Radio smashed a copy of 'Fight For Your Right' on air in a gesture of ludicrously heavy outrage; the *Mirror* took their pop columnist at her word and came out editorially against The Beastie Boys, actually going so far as to recommend that CBS drop them from their roster forthwith. CBS were probably too busy dealing with all the death threats which were piling up as a result of the Mirror article. Hotels came out in force against them. And as the tour headed inexorably towards its last date, at Liverpool's Royal Court theatre, the press campaign reached an astonishing level of hatred.

The Liverpool gig, inevitably, ended in a full-scale riot. This time The Beastie Boys, in a perverted way, got their wish, and the show was an apocalypse. No need anymore for the semi-naked girls in cages, no need for the beer-fights and abuse. Here was teargas, here was alleged grievous bodily harm.

What seems to have happened is that local Liverpool thugs, provoked into action by Beastie Boy notoriety, took it upon themselves to attend the concert and salvage some glory for old Britannia, or failing that to give the Beasties a good hiding. A barrage of beer cans hurtled towards the stage, so many that AdRock was moved to throw some back. He also wielded a baseball bat. After a matter of minutes the show was stopped when a teargas canister emptied the hall.

While The Beastie Boys high-tailed it back to London their expensive equipment was wrecked (not being musicians themselves they relied on mixing desks and turntables) and chants of victory à la football matches were heard from sections of the crowd. Five people were arrested after the show, and in an amazing dénouement to the story AdRock was arrested at his London hotel and charged with grievous bodily harm. A female fan had allegedly been hit in the face by a beer can thrown back into the audience by the singer.

Suddenly the joke wasn't funny anymore, if it ever was. The irreverent Beastie philosophy ('Basically we make sexist, drunk records') seemed grim and loathsome and, in the words of The Sex Pistols and Ronnie Biggs, both of whom really ought to know, 'No-one is innocent'.

AdRock was found not guilty in November 1987, after the charge had been changed to actual bodily harm. The girl who brought the charges announced that she would not accept the verdict, and would not let the matter drop. Meanwhile AdRock

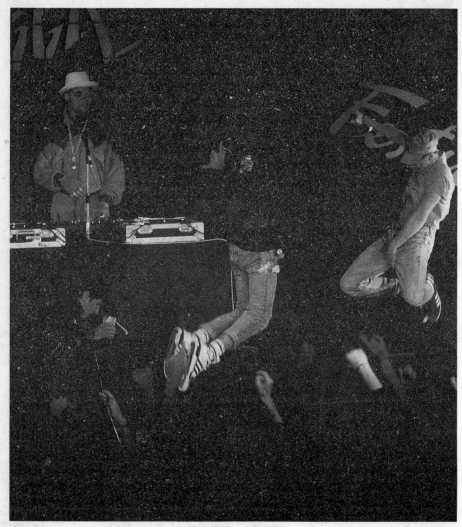

The Beastie Boys

sought the company of 'Brat Pack' actress Molly Ringwald.

And now all that remains of The Beastie Boys is a gap left on the bonnet of an occasional Volkswagen. The craze for wearing VW logos round the neck as medallions developed into an alarming phenomenon for the company. Once the first kid was prosecuted for obtaining one illegally, the demand for them became incredible. So, in a gesture of goodwill, Volkswagen started giving them away for free.

# Paul McCartney is Dead

One of the principal effects of The Beatles' decision not to play any more concerts after 1966 was that the public had a vital dimension to their hero worship snatched away. Sure, The Beatles were in the studio making their finest records, and could be glimpsed occasionally emerging bleary-eyed from some session or other. But it wasn't the same. The Beatles weren't *visible* any more. They couldn't be monitored like before. And that is how, towards the end of the Sixties, the rumour began to spread, in all its absurd, malevolent glory, that Paul McCartney was dead.

Or to be perfectly precise, that Paul McCartney had been killed in a car crash in November 1966. The implications of this were fairly obvious, such as who exactly was that playing the terrific bass lines on 'With A Little Help From My Friends' and 'Penny Lane', and how come his mysterious successor had a dead ringer of a voice?

Assuming that Paul McCartney is still very much alive, which seems like a pretty sensible assumption to make, an analysis of the so-called 'proof' of his untimely demise will give some idea of not only the frightening intensity of Beatlemania, but also the lunatic edge of the Sixties.

The story was supposedly started in America by a college paper. Pretty soon it made a local radio station, and on the basis of the no-smoke-without-fire rule, spread across the States.

The car crash story started when it was discovered that an accident of the kind described in the rumour had taken place around the time specified. One of the two fatally injured passengers was a young man with dark hair. He had been disfigured beyond all recognition.

Another fact which lent credence to the rumour was that The Beatles had held a McCartney lookalike competition in 1966. This now took on a vaguely disturbing angle – were they in fact searching, under the guise of a good-natured contest, for a replacement for their dead bass player? It seemed plausible at the time, especially when it was discovered that no announcement had ever been made regarding any winner of the contest.

The story circulated that a young Scotsman named William Campbell had replaced McCartney and had been playing on recordings by the group since 1966. Their retirement from concert appearances meant that nobody could twig that it was a bogus Paul.

In the crazy logic of the best rumours, the treasure hunt did not end there. For the story went that The Beatles were so contrite at having duped their fans that, towards the end of the Sixties, they began to put clues on the sleeves of their albums and into their lyrics. These clues, when deciphered and compiled, added up to indisputable proof that Paul McCartney was dead. That was the theory.

The 'clues' started as far back as the song 'Yellow Submarine'. Dating from the year 1966, this song is a mildly controversial one even without shadowy undertones of possible death mentioned in the grooves – its childish ditty format is reckoned to mask one of John Lennon's most enthusiastic drug songs. As regards the Paul rumour, the story had it that at one point in the song Lennon shouts out 'Paul's a queer', the object being to instigate a smear campaign against McCartney so that fans would not feel too bad when they learned that he was actually brown bread.

Two more 'clues' in the lyrics of songs fuelled the rumours. One is fairly obvious – the line in 'A Day In The Life' which runs 'he blew his mind out in a car'. It is now widely believed that this refers to Tara Browne, the heir to the Guinness fortunes, who died in a car crash just before recording for the song commenced. The other clue is more obscure. Apparently there is a spoken line in the lengthy fade out on 'Strawberry Fields Forever' which goes 'I buried Paul'. Others have since argued that it is Lennon saying 'Cranberry sauce'. This, on the face of it, seems more likely. However, there remains the possibility that, having sung all the words to 'Strawberry Fields', he is in fact complaining to the other Beatles, 'I'm very hoarse'.

The remainder of the evidence lies in the sleeves of the LPs released by The Beatles between the years 1967 and 1969. The first one of these, *Sgt. Pepper's Lonely Hearts Club Band*, boasts an impressive pop-art mural of celebrities and statesmen, with the four Beatles at the front of the throng. Look closely and one can see a 'wreath' of flowers arranged in the shape of a bass guitar. Squint at the flowers and they appear to read PAUL? This was taken to mean a question mark hanging over McCartney's existence. The raised hand at the back of Paul's head on the front cover is supposedly an Indian death sign. But for proof positive, eager theoreticians gestured excitedly to the inner sleeve – there was the reputedly alive 'n' kicking bassist wearing a badge with the damning initials OPD. Could this mean anything other than Officially Pronounced Dead?

Yes. It could stand for Ontario Police Department, where he was given the badge.

The rumour-mongers were not deterred. All the walrus symbolism of the *Magical Mystery Tour* LP (apart from the song 'I Am The Walrus' on the record, Paul is dressed like one on the cover) was taken to mean a death obsession, for no other reason than that a walrus in *Alice In Wonderland* killed a few oysters. But, there again, was a raised hand behind McCartney's head. Twice, in the accompanying booklet.

The transitional *Yellow Submarine* soundtrack album fared no better. Yet again Paul McCartney was seen with a hand raised above his head.

However, it was the cover of *Abbey Road* that sent the really inventive scandal hunters into paroxysms of creativity. The four Beatles were crossing Abbey Road in north London in what appeared to more sensitive eyes to be a mock funeral procession. John Lennon, at the head of the procession and dressed in white, was the preacher. Ringo, lagging behind but still smartly attired, was the mourner. George, in casual clothes and languishing at the back, was the gravedigger. And Paul was the corpse. Look – not only was he quite clearly dead, he was also not wearing any shoes. And everyone knows that most countries bury their dead barefoot.

A Volkswagen car parked in the middle distance was taken as an important clue. Its registration number reads, in part, 281F. Keen – but erroneous – mathematicians calculated that McCartney's age in the year of *Abbey Road*'s release would have been 28 IF he had lived. Actually, being of 1942 vintage, Paul would have been 27. But then it was remembered that The Beatles were heavily into Eastern mysticism, and those religions believe that everybody is born one year old. Suddenly it made sense.

Ironically, the treasure hunters missed the most blatant and irrefutable clue of all. During the fade out of 'Back In The USSR', the first song on the 'White Album', John Lennon can be heard quite clearly speaking the words, ''Ere, Yoko, 'ave this bass. Paul won't need it where 'e's goin'.'

# Preacher Man

## Little Richard

Richard, who wasn't all *that* little, not when he piled up his pompadour and stood atop his piano, came from the sour segregated heart of Georgia. He hit it off instantly with the church, where his large family ued to sing gospel songs.

He was a peculiar kid. For a start he had one leg much shorter than the other, which made him walk oddly. And for another thing, he was well versed in sodomy by the age of 13. The local kids were suspicious of him, this shrill-voiced phenomenon who always wanted to be the mommy when they played house.

He had his first break in show business when a travelling show came to Georgia and picked him up. They named him Little Richard (he was still only 14) and took him on the road. During the late Forties and early Fifties he built something of a reputation for himself, with a succession of different shows, and in 1951 he got a chance to record.

The result, 'Every Hour', was a local hit in Georgia. But then Richard's father, Bud Penniman, was shot dead in an argument and Richard had to take a job washing dishes to support his family.

This was only a temporary setback, however, and a passing promoter persuaded him to play again. His next recordings hinted at the rock 'n' roll ecstasy that was to come, but lacked the rawness of his classic recordings. As something of a last resort he made a demo tape and sent it off to a label in Los Angeles called Specialty. Months later he got a call.

He came to record a session for Specialty and, truth to tell, most of the stuff was pretty dire. It was only on one song that he shone. This was a vaguely obscene ditty that he liked to warble as he progressed through life. 'If it don't fit, don't force it', he used to sing, 'you can grease it, make it easy.' The lyrics were toned down for general consumption by a New Orleans songwriter and the result sounded somewhat like a mother hyena singing

Little Richard

a song to her children. 'A wop bop aloo bop a wop bam boom/Tutti Frutti/Aw rootie/Tutti Frutti/Aw rootie'.

'Tutti Frutti', the song Little Richard least expected to be a hit, delighted the radio stations and got him 'white' as well as 'black' airplay. Even though the lyrics had been expurgated, the intent was there – it was pure sexual energy disguised as comedy. In 1955 that sold you approximately half a million records.

Then something began which was to dog Richard all his life. At that time it was usual for black singers to have their songs covered by whites (usually in inferior versions) and sit back and watch the limp, emasculated cover climb the charts. 'Tutti Frutti' was given to Pat Boone, a profound white churchgoer, who brought an earnest quality to the song that made it laughable.

Reasoning, correctly, that Boone would also take a stab at recording Richard's follow-up, Specialty released 'Long Tall Sally', a frenetic blur of a song that nobody could decipher, let alone sing along to. Boone did cover it, but he didn't sound like he was enjoying the experience.

The Little Richard image was unprecedented in rock 'n' roll. He would wear mascara to accentuate his eyes, sequins and diamonds all over his suits, and he would leap, jump and cartwheel at his piano. The audiences, given carte blanche, would go wild. Screaming, heaving, pulsating crowds torched into life by this ridiculous, almost threateningly effeminate figure from the South. It became a tradition for the girls at the front to jettison their underwear at Richard and his band.

He was also bringing the races together, without really looking like he meant to. Integrated audiences could partake of Little Richard. It was not as though he belonged to either colour, just as he was cool and liberal with his body.

This was leading him towards a major dilemma. On the one hand, he got off on the attentions of the girls, and it wasn't as though he was indulging in the inevitable after-show orgies against his will. But the influence of the church had never left him. And something in the beat of his music worried him. Something told him it might actually be the rhythm of the devil. He couldn't be sure, but he knew he had to do something.

On a tour of Australia Richard evidently had a terrifying vision of the Apocalypse. He took a plane ride soon after and happened to glance out the window. Mistaking the engine exhaust smoke for a terrible fire, he prayed to the Lord that the plane would not crash, promising to do His work and give up the debaucheries and wealth of the rock 'n' roll business. The Lord clearly knew a bargain when he heard one and the plane landed safely. (Richard later admitted that he could have been wrong about the fire.)

The result was the retirement of the most flamboyant figure the business had ever seen. The jewellery went into Sydney Harbour, the limos went in the garage and Richard went into a bible school to get it together with the scriptures.

The rumours questioned his sanity. Richard's cracked, the press surmised. All that pressure's finally gotten to him. Some reports had him banged up in an asylum. Others had him commit suicide, convinced that he was evil.

What he did do was get married, to a secretary from Washington whom he met at an evangelical meeting. Richard was not the marrying kind, however, and the union was doomed right from the start. He was not completely cut off from the rock 'n' roll lifestyle, however, and he still liked to roll up for bible classes in his yellow Cadillac. He went back into the recording studio, this time to make an album of sacred songs. It was snapped up by the public, although what they thought of it is a matter for some conjecture.

Then Richard was arrested for loitering in a public toilet for anti-social and illegal purposes, and his wife filed for divorce. The lure of his old lifestyle was pulling him back, and in 1962 he agreed to do a gospel tour of England.

What he had not been told was that it was a rock 'n' roll tour, and that the folks in England don't as a rule expect rock musicians to preach the gospel.

After performing his gospel set to almost total silence, Richard then had to go through the agony of watching Sam Cooke steal his audience with the sort of no-holds-barred shaman showmanship he had been famous for. Richard strolled back onstage with his band and tore the place apart with 'Long Tall Sally'.

The resurrection was not, however, a total one. He still felt the pull of the church. And it was not until 1964 when, distressed at the British Invasion or maybe inspired by it, he made his official rock 'n' roll comeback. He failed miserably. He had left it too late. There was quite obviously no religious message in 'Bama Lama Bama Loo', but none of his fans wanted to know. Tastes were different now – it was The Beatles and The Stones who ripped up halls and left the girls for dead, and Richard seemed like an uninspired old curio.

The comeback attempts never quite ceased, but they slowed down for long periods. The cocaine flirtations became a habit, the zest of irrepressible youth became wheezing middle age, and Richard saw out 1977, the year of punk rock, radical chic and dress sense even more cathartic than his own, as a bible salesman.

# Al Green

Al Green was a sugar-voiced soul singer of the Seventies whose vocal insinuations often challenged listeners to guess exactly what sex he was. He had a string of hits from 1971's 'Tired Of Being Alone' through the next four years, and many of his songs including 'Let's Stay Together', 'Take Me To The River' and 'L.O.V.E.' have been successfully covered by other artists.

Behind the super-cool façade that spelled sexual gratification, supreme confidence and down-home charm lay a much more complex and diffident human being. The fantasy image some fans had of him was often hopelessly misplaced.

One such fan, a 29-year-old woman named Mary Woodson, approached Green with a view to marrying him. She soon found that all her ideals had been gleaned from his vinyl performances and were therefore not to be trusted. She was persistent, however, and forced Green into a situation where he had to reject her.

In retaliation she threw a pot of scalding grits down his back (the Alabama-raised Green must have appreciated the symbolism of *that*) and then shot herself. Al Green's career hit a temporary hiatus while he recovered. When he resumed singing it was in a much more religious vein, almost as though he were looking for the guidance to come to terms with the incident, as well as a reason for it happening. He is now a preacher.

# SHEER HEART ATTACK

## Paul Kossoff

In the mid-Sixties in England there was an upsurge of interest in blues music, and with it came a gaggle of heroic middle class guitarists to interpret the solos and cadences of the music. Jeff Beck, Jimmy Page and Eric Clapton all survived anonymous Home Counties upbringings and sallied forth into worlds of pain, fatigue and staggering excess. In 1968 they were followed by a young man named Paul Kossoff.

Paul Kossoff was the son of the moderately famous English actor David Kossoff. Paul was born in 1950 and soon developed an aptitude for the guitar. The blues fixation came with a visit to a London club to see the Sixties' prime exponents of British blues, John Mayall's Bluesbreakers. Mayall had an obsession about the blues which never quite became accessible enough for public tastes. But his group served as a nursery for three of the best guitarists of the British rock scene – Peter Green, Mick Taylor, and the man Paul Kossoff saw that night in 1965, Eric Clapton.

It has been argued eloquently that the blues is by its very nature a black man's form, and that white exponents thereof are inevitably going to sound unconvincing and patronizing. One listen to Eric Clapton's solo on 'All Your Love' on the *Bluesbreakers* album will make a nonsense of that argument. If that is what convinced Kossoff that he should be playing the blues, his later recordings with Free suggested that the groundwork had already been done deep inside him.

Kossoff's first band, Black Cat Bones, was one of a merry thousand similar bands doing the blues appreciation number up and down the country in the late Sixties. The one interesting thing about them was the personal feeling their young guitarist was able to invest in standards that had been written before he had been born.

In 1968 he and the drummer, Simon Kirke, left in search of a slightly more original statement. They formed a band with the help of blues champion and musician/broadcaster Alexis Korner, who put them in touch with a singer called Paul Rodgers and a brilliant bassist called Andy Fraser, who had been thrown out of John Mayall's Bluesbreakers for the cardinal sin of being only 15.

Korner named them Free (their first producer wanted to call them The Heavy Metal Kids) and they began a seven nights a week lifestyle that honed them into a genuinely inspiring band. The average age of Free in 1968 was 18. In other circumstances the epithet 'teenie boppers' would have been hard to dislodge, but the seriousness with which Free approached their music staved off any cynical criticisms.

Their first two albums, in 1968 and 1969, were raw, youthful creations which failed to sway the masses to the desired degree. However, their third single, 'All Right Now', was a huge hit and stands 18 years later as one of the classic rock songs to come from this country. It catapulted the four members of Free – average age by now a mature 20 – into the big time.

The pressures of stardom, to say nothing of the pressures of repeating this success, found their most vulnerable victim in Paul Kossoff. He lived the myth of the blues guitarist in all its fragmented glory and indulged cheerfully in drugs. This disturbed the other members of the band; rifts ensued and when the single 'The Stealer' failed to follow 'All Right Now' to the dizzy heights the band split up in acrimony.

Kossoff was particularly badly hit by the split. His recording career did not depend totally on Free, for he was a much-courted session lead guitarist, but when the fame stopped dead it pushed him further into drugs.

After a temporary separation Free re-formed without Fraser, who was replaced by the Japanese bassist Tetsu Yamauchi. The hope was that by getting Free back together again, they could all get Kossoff back together again.

Sadly, it didn't work. After playing on the reunion album, *Free At Last* Kossoff sought immediate oblivion and declared himself unavailable for the imminent Japanese tour.

On a subsequent British tour some dates had to be cancelled when Kossoff, supposedly stoned out of his mind, tripped on some cables and injured himself. It was well known now that he was taking heroin.

On the next, and last, Free album he played guitar on only a handful of songs and when the time came to tour again a replacement guitarist was drafted in. Kossoff, crushed, retreated even more. Heroin and mandrax cushioned him in his little Notting Hill flat. He refused to have anything to do with his family.

Around this time – 1973 – he made a depressingly inconclusive solo album called *Back Street Crawler*. The following year he hardly picked up a guitar.

In 1975 he seemed to have snapped out of it when he announced the formation of a new road band called Back Street Crawler. A nine-date tour resulted but proved nothing more than that Free had been a great band. The BSC album *The Band Played On* was an even starker deal. One of the problems was that Kossoff was never a writer. Other than a few co-credits he never wrote for Free, and the BSC material was out of his hands too.

Paul Kossoff had a massive heart attack in September 1975 and spent his 25th birthday in hospital. He was technically dead for 35 seconds before doctors managed to restart his heart. Against all advice he launched himself into BSC dates and fears seemed justified when he made an extremely ropey appearance on the BBC's Old Grey Whistle Test.

In November 1975 a BSC tour, dramatically curtailed, saw the artistic demise of Paul Kossoff. At Glasgow's Apollo he stumbled around playing out of tune, until eventually he fell over. Some of the crowd were seen to be in tears.

March 1976 saw some good news at last. He went to America to have discussions with Atlantic Records. Tragically, on a flight from Los Angeles to New York he died in his sleep. It was a recurrence of his heart condition which caused his death. He was 25.

His father had been planning a tour of his one-man performances for charities. It was supposed to be his way of saying thank you for his son's life having been spared in September. The tour went ahead, with David Kossoff reading some touching thoughts on his dead son, whom he described as a 'young blues guitarist'.

# Jim Morrison

'There's the known. And there's the unknown. And what separates them is the door, and that's what I want to be. I want to be the door.' – Jim Morrison, 1967.

There is a man living in the Amazonian rainforests who has one hell of a past, should he care to own up to it.

Or, alternatively, there is a bath tub in a flat in Paris that could tell a few stories.

Nobody knows what happened on the night of 2 July 1971; nobody who is alive today saw Jim Morrison's dead body. All that is known for certain is that during his 27 years on the earth he changed forever the way rock music is presented on stage, totally redefined the concept of rock singer as messiah to a subservient generation, and completely rewrote the book on the matter of rock lyrics.

As a poet in a bluesy, gutsy rock group, as a melodramatic and dangerous performer, as a tortured artist, he appeared to be the god of several different religions, all committed to the same goal: 'the breaking away or overthrowing of established order . . . revolt, chaos, especially activity that seems to have no meaning.'

James Douglas Morrison was born on 8 December 1943, in Florida, the son of a fastidiously upright high-ranking naval officer. A hyperactive, intelligent child, the young Jim bewildered his peers and thrilled his teachers by quoting extensively from Joyce, Kerouac and Nietzsche while still in high school. His genius IQ and craving for the classics went hand in hand with a magnetic personality. Pretty soon he was engaging in verbal duels with his English teacher.

A keen writer himself, he was a sucker for the Rimbaud legend. Rimbaud had written all his poetry by the end of his teens and vanished into a life of slave trading in Africa. He had also put forth the increasingly popular proposition that the true poet – as opposed to the would-be poet – must risk personal ruin on every level in order to stand a realistic chance of seeing the unknown, the mad, the beautiful.

Turned on to rock music by friends at UCLA, where he was studying cinematography, Morrison started to set his words to music. He met up with organist Ray Manzarek, and the latter's reaction – 'Those are the greatest lyrics I've ever heard' – propelled them both into a serious rock career. The whole thing gelled when guitarist Robbie Krieger and drummer John Densmore enlisted. In 1965 The Doors began to play in public.

Months of rehearsals and useful practice gigs in deserted bars helped to perfect the act. In it the hitherto-shy Morrison, skinned down to a lean, confident ten stones, was behaving increasingly dramatically, serving up his lyrics with theatrical moves and overt, sexual poses. He began to consider very seriously the role of poet/leader/visionary, and gobbled tabs of LSD to open up a few more doors. Lest the American interest in matters Vietnamese put a dampener on the exciting new proceedings, Morrison pleaded homosexuality to dodge the draft.

The blatant sexuality of his stage act in the formative months, which called for maximum friction between groin and microphone stand, was offset by the epic soundscapes that The Doors were building around his lyrics. Morrison's obsessions with potent poetic images – sex, death, fire, speed, intimacy and distance, reptiles, violence and love – were pretty articulate for one so possessed. What he was screaming had meaning. At this point the audience hysteria was a source of inspiration to him. Later he would be repulsed by it.

The Doors' most traumatic song at this stage was called 'The End'. It included an approximation of the Oedipal conflict, in which Morrison sang – or screamed – the following words:

And he came to a door
And he looked inside.
'Father.'
'Yes, son?'
'I want to kill you.'
'Mother!'
'I want to ffffuuuuuuuuuuuuuuuck-youuuuuuuuuuuuu.'

The Doors' eponymous debut album was a mighty triumph on its release in 1967, and necessitated some sort of hackneyed biography for magazines to quote from. Bored with the usual 'favourite colour' scenario, Morrison cobbled together a few random notes along with scant biographical histories of the four Doors. He described his own attitude to being in the Doors as 'the feeling of a bow string being pulled back for 22 years and suddenly let go'. Further down the page he claimed that his parents were dead.

As the focal point of the band, Morrison's life was becoming more and more complex. A natural drinker, one who drinks to drink rather than to socialize, he started to knock back greater and greater quantities of liquor, mixing it with perilous wedges of dope and frequent acid excursions. He was fairly settled into a relationship with a girlfriend, Pamela Courson, but enjoyed outbreaks of promiscuity.

The faster the rollercoaster, the more he drank to stay in focus. Drink gradually usurped drugs. One night he visited Jac Holzman, the head of his record label Elektra, and threw up all over his front porch. It was a common occurrence for him to go on stage tanked to the limit. Every night a different binge.

An incident in New Haven, Connecticut, towards the end of 1968 marked a swift decline in the quality of Doors performances. An argument backstage with a particularly unartistic cop resulted in Morrison being sprayed in the face with a can of mace. Morrison proceeded to relate the story on stage, suitably embellished, and was arrested for a breach of the peace.

Already exhibiting impatience with the mindless, stoned teenagers who he felt were desecrating the performances, he treated his audiences with more and more contempt, attempting to spur them into some kind of action, even if it had to be violent and negative.

Meanwhile his drinking had reached saturation level. His fridge had been stripped of food in order to accommodate more beer and he was banned from several bars in the Los Angeles area, where the group was based. He seemed to be drunk all the time. At a recording session for the song 'The Unknown Soldier' he needed 130 takes before he got it right.

His hatred of blanket audience conformity drove him over the edge. Being obviously drunk hadn't moved

Jim Morrison's grave

them, spitting at them hadn't moved them, and swearing at them had only excited them. He resolved to put into action a plan he had conceived many years before. He would instigate a riot, then stand back and observe at first hand the gut reactions of the rabble.

It is quite easy for a rock band to start a riot. All one has to do is play one's most provocative material very quickly, without a break, while raising personal hell up there on stage.

Therefore, one night in Chicago, Morrison deliberately cued in the revolutionary 'The Unknown Soldier', the inflammatory 'Five To One' and the cataclysmic 'When The Music's Over'. All the while he gyrated to the music in a display of such terminal anguish that the audience charged the stage the minute he left it.

Encouraged by the toadying attentions of his entourage, he began to behave in arch poetic style – as practised years earlier by Dylan Thomas and Brendan Behan, to the detriment of both – and drank himself under every available table, emerging only to vomit or hassle some pretty waitress. His looks suffered, his weight shot up and, worst of all, his voice deteriorated.

The second riot came in New York. This time he went straight for the jugular. Right from the beginning of the set he did his epileptic contortionist's dance, clamping one fist on his crotch, the other on the microphone, writhing on the stage in a state of frenzied ecstasy. The result was a pitched battle between police

and audience when the kids attempted to envelop the crazy man on stage.

He explained away the riots in playful fashion: 'We have fun. The kids have fun. The cops have fun.'

Still, the riots were becoming just another expected facet of The Doors' stage act. No longer were they a novelty. There was a depressing 'roll up, roll up, come and see the freaks' attitude in the minds of the kids.

Morrison felt that he had resolved the dilemma when he came into contact with a radical drama group called The Living Theatre. They were getting into areas of direct confrontation, using shock tactics like nudity and repetition to stun the audience and slap them out of their complacency. Morrison was starting to assimilate these ideas, wondering how to introduce them into a Doors show.

The fact that he failed miserably was put down at the time to alcohol, but it remains an extremely grey area. What he did in an effort to move a crowd was a depressing display of at worst egotistical machismo, at best puerile petulance. Faced, in Miami, with a typically stultifying audience, he resorted as usual to some preliminary abuse:

'You are all a bunch of fucking idiots. Your faces are being pressed into the shit of the world. Take your fucking friend and love him. Do you want to see my cock?'

He then, it was alleged, 'did lewdly and lasciviously expose his penis in a vulgar or indecent manner with intent to be observed, did place his hand on the penis and shake it, and further . . . did simulate the acts of masturbation upon himself and oral copulation upon another.'

Although he did not know it at the time, there was a warrant out for his arrest.

The hell-raising did not abate. A film he had an idea for went to the rehearsal stage. One scene involved him dancing along a 17th floor ledge without a safety net. He did this, despite the howling protests of friends, and finished by urinating down to the street below.

The Doors were now about as popular as Henry VIII in a singles' bar. The remaining gigs on their schedule were cancelled by the local authorities for fear of further riots, and they only managed to secure immediate work by agreeing to what Morrison called a 'fuck clause' – in other words, one hint of an unzipped fly and the cops get to join in on the chorus.

While awaiting trial for the events in Miami, Morrison was arrested a second time, for being drunk and disorderly on an airplane. In the wake of various hi-jacking attempts, security around airports had tightened and this was now a very serious charge. It was compounded by a new charge, 'interfering with the flight of an aircraft'. The offence carried ten years.

He was a wreck by now, unstable, teetering. He no longer bothered to find a toilet when he needed to pee. Just used the carpet. A lucky break at the 'hi-jacking' trial – the key witness

didn't recognize him – took care of one legal matter. But the Miami affair was still outstanding and it seemed likely that no amount of hip legal rhetoric from the Morrison camp would be able to persuade the judge that Jim Morrison was actually bang in tune with the mores of the time.

In the meantime he married a witch. She was called Patricia Kennely and she edited one of Morrison's favourite American rock papers. In a formal witches' wedding, they signed their names in their own blood.

The Miami affair came to trial. Seventeen prosecution witnesses of pristine, virginal disposition took the oath and claimed to have been outraged/shocked/disgusted by Morrison's behaviour on the night of the alleged offences.

He was found guilty, to nobody's surprise, of profanity and indecent exposure. The sentence was six months in jail and a $500 fine. An appeal was lodged.

Morrison had been getting heavily into cocaine. His love of the quick high, the delirious rush, was satisfied perfectly by the effects of this drug, and he combined it with alcohol to produce a state of heightened neutralized glee.

Around this time he was approached by members of an anti-drug campaign and asked to record a personalized message warning his impressionable teenage fans about the dangers of speed.

'Hello . . .' he began, 'this is Jim Morrison of The Doors. I just want to tell you that shooting speed ain't cool . . . so snort it.'

Taking a major breather from the band, the trials, and all his worries, Morrison fled to Europe with his on-off girlfriend Pamela. He never returned.

On Monday, 5 July 1971, several calls were put through to the English offices of Elektra Records. Everybody wanted to know the same thing – was it true that Jim Morrison was dead?

The calls were shrugged off. It was perfectly in the nature of things to dodge rumours of Morrison's tragic demise. It happened every time he went on a weekend binge. The rumours, however, were gathering pace and this time there was no Morrison in the office to nullify them. So The Doors' manager called Pamela in Paris and received an oddly muted instruction to come over as soon as possible. Arriving the following day he found the flat; in it he found Pamela, a sealed coffin and a signed death certificate attributing the death of James Douglas Morrison to a heart attack. The coffin was interred the following day.

Immediately the stories began to circulate. It was pointed out that Pamela was the only one who saw the body – apart from the doctor who signed the death certificate, and he couldn't be found. Suspicions were aroused that Morrison could have suffered anything so, well, mundane as a heart attack.

Jim Morrison died in a bath tub. This happens to be the common place for victims of a heroin overdose to end up (in the hope that the water will shock them back to life). Morrison had been seen hanging around notorious Parisian heroin dealers in the days leading up to his death. To this day Paris believes that Morrison died of an overdose.

The only one who could have settled the matter once and for all is now no longer in a position to do so: Pamela died in 1974.

Therefore, it is a case of whom you believe: a qualified Parisian doctor, albeit one who ran to ground and stayed there; the woman who was virtually his wife; or a few close friends who were privy to Morrison's most bitter attacks on the music business and the unspeakable evil of the dumb Pavlovian audiences. And they mention the marvellous, madcap plan he thought up one day as far back as 1967 – how, when it all got too hectic and too useless, he'd relocate to the jungle, lose his bearings in the new sensations and gradually forget the bad times. Then, when he was good and ready, he would make contact with his friends again, using the cryptic nom-de-guerre Mr Mojo Risin . . . which crossword lovers will instantly recognize as an anagram of Jim Morrison.

# OLDIES...

Phil Spector

# Phil Spector

The facts about Phil Spector are easy enough to catalogue – but they make fairly astounding reading when you take into account his age and lack of experience, his small stature and his high-pitched voice. Never has such a blatantly inconsequential guy done so much. Well, at least, not since the mad heyday of Napoleon Bonaparte.

The facts are that, at age 17, he had already had a hit record. This was 'To Know Him Is To Love Him', an achingly tender love song recorded with loads of echo and credited to The Teddy Bears. Actually, apart from the sincere high school warbling of chanteuse Annette Kleinbard, the record was all Spector's. He wrote it, he sang on it, he played on it, he shared in its production. He even dreamed up the title, after reading similar words on his father's gravestone. In 1958 the 17-year-old Spector was already semi-legendary, incurring the wrath of all who met him due to his eccentricity and directness.

Three years later he was producing records regularly, with little success, but he was getting his name around. Three years after *that*, at the age of 23, he was the Tycoon Of Teen, producer of glorious teen laments like 'Be My Baby', 'Da Doo Ron Ron' and 'He's A Rebel', all delivered in Spector's customized 'Wall Of Sound', a studio technique whereby each record sounded as though three entire orchestras were playing on it.

The hits became longer, braver and greater. The Righteous Brothers' 'You've Lost That Lovin' Feeling' from 1965 could be called with some justification the most utterly perfect single of all time. 'Baby I Love You' was a huge hit for The Ronettes, the buxom, dark-eyed trio fashioned around Veronica Spector, Phil's wife. Then, in 1966, the industry hit back for what it saw as Spector's failure to pay his dues. All along he had played the game his way, as though rules were tiresome peripherals to be negotiated and ultimately forgotten about. He ignored the radio stations, believing (correctly) that his records were the best, so obviously they would get airplay. He was outspoken and ungrateful. Worse still, he was the very antithesis of the shy, retiring aw-shucks-it-was-nothing types much beloved of the music industry in the States at the time. After making an uncomplimentary comment about radio programmers on a TV documentary, he fell from grace with an almighty bang.

The rejection, when it arrived, came in ludicrous form. His masterwork, Ike and Tina Turner's 'River Deep, Mountain High' was not a hit. It entered the US charts at 88 and dropped straight out again. As it is now reckoned to be one of Spector's greatest achievements (as was his achievement of keeping Ike Turner off the record for fear of losing control over it), it stunned his friends. Its failure was variously laughed off, explained away with references to bad vocal mixes and so on, and most commonly justified by the assertion that Phil Spector had simply gone too far. It was, for what it's worth, a monstrous hit in Britain.

Spector retired from the music business, a crushed man, no longer interested in creating his complex 'teen symphonies'. He disappeared for more than two years, some say into the desert, and while he was gone the rumours about him started . . .

Legend had it that the reason Phil Spector was so tough and uncompromising was solely due to his height, or lack thereof. An incident from his early career brought his shortcomings sharply into focus. After a Teddy Bears show, Spector went to the lavatory and was followed in by four men who had seen the show and been less than overwhelmed. They locked the doors, opened their collective trouserage, and pissed all over the legend of Phillip Spector. He vowed, according to close friends, that this would 'never happen again'.

That is how the bodyguard obsession started – he was genuinely terrified of physical conflict.

He had been no stranger to controversy in the years before the hit flood began. Growing his hair to extraordinary lengths, even before The Beatles touched down in America and led the hirsute revolution, he also used to dress in sinister black cloaks, earning the nickname 'D'Artagnan'.

There was also the matter of the third single by his group The Crystals. They had been his first protégées, scoring reasonable hits in early 1962. Their latest single would be a song called 'He Hit Me (And It Felt Like A Kiss)'. In the song, which is in actual fact quite a happy little tune because the assailant and his hapless girlfriend make up and live to fight another day, the female singer provides a sulking commentary which was understandably mistaken for sado-masochism at the time. Listeners switched off in droves and the record was swiftly withdrawn.

After the mighty 'You've Lost That Lovin' Feeling' ('our Cilla' did a cover version of the song in Britain, cutting 40 seconds off it because she 'didn't want people to get bored'), Spector's fears and phobias took a turn for the worse. He developed a terror of airplanes, often getting off at the last minute before take-off because he was convinced it was going to crash.

Then there was the time he bought Lenny Bruce's negatives. Bruce, a risqué comedian whose persecution by the establishment turned him into first a junkie and then a corpse, died with a syringe stuck in his arm. Spector paid $5,000 in 1966 for the police negatives.

Spector returned in early 1969 with a couple of half-hearted hits. He then began a long and fruitful association with two of The Beatles, George Harrison and John Lennon. This stemmed from his rescue-production job on The Beatles' last album, *Let It*

*Be*, which was lambasted by, among others, Paul McCartney. Spector was the producer of Harrison's single 'My Sweet Lord', a fairly innocuous albeit uplifting record which was the subject of a court case when it was found to bear compositional similarities to a song by The Chiffons, 'He's So Fine'. (Interestingly enough, in 1976 Jonathan King, whose records tended to lampoon rather than plagiarise, included a version of 'He's So Fine' on his album *J.K. All The Way*, set to the tune of 'My Sweet Lord', complete with Harrison guitar solo impersonations and sporadic namechecks of Harrison songs such as 'Something' and 'Here Comes The Sun'.) The irony is that when Harrison lost the case the man to whom he had to pay the damages was Allen Klein, the man whom Harrison was content to have as manager of The Beatles post-Epstein.

In April 1974 a story in the American press alleged that Phil Spector had been involved in a serious car crash travelling between Los Angeles and Phoenix. The car exploded into flames and Spector suffered multiple head injuries and severe burns. Several operations later, his press office did not seem to know exactly if he was getting better or not.

Spector recovered enough to produce Leonard Cohen's album *Death Of A Ladies' Man*, during which the story goes that he kept Cohen in the studio at gunpoint until the album was finished. That reminded the aficionados of classic Spector behaviour, like when he insisted on monitoring Veronica's calls back in the Sixties and refused to allow her to leave the grounds of the mansion in Hollywood where they lived, even threatening to kill her and keep her in a glass coffin. And the time when he pulled a gun on Stevie Wonder. And the time when he turned up at the Whisky A Go-Go and screamed so hard he had to be carried out.

If Spector stands accused of wanting the earth, all of it, right now, then he is also guilty of being a genius with malice aforethought. We don't need to know what he is up to now – every time 'Da Doo Ron Ron' comes on the radio, that's enough. His projects now are pretty insubstantial. In 1980 he produced The Ramones, a bunch of committed Spectorites from the wrong side of the tracks. One song, 'Rock 'n' Roll High School' opens with a loud, effective, crashing guitar chord. It's the sort of thing Johnny Ramone plays in his sleep. Spector spent hours, days playing it back, adding to it, subtracting from it, mating it with itself until he eventually had it. Triumphantly he played it to the band. Johnny shrugged. It was *okay* . . . but wasn't it exactly the same as when he had played it?

# The Mamas And The Papas

The pretty harmonies of The Mamas And The Papas hid a multitude of personal and narcotic sins, only really brought to the public's consciousness on the publication of John Phillips's extraordinary memoirs in the mid-Eighties. Although they were essentially a folk group, singing intricate four-part vocal harmonies to create an often spellbinding whole, they were caught up in the superstardom channels of the mid-Sixties and they never really recovered.

The fact that the excess continued well into the Seventies and even into the Eighties is a testament both to the fact that friendships made in the Sixties are not easy to shake off, and that for a disturbingly large amount of people fame is something to be grasped at with clammy, desperate hands. Take that fame away and you are often left with a fierce drug habit.

Like many American kids of the Sixties, John Phillips was primed for performing after witnessing Elvis on the Ed Sullivan Show. Except that Phillips was no longer a kid. He had been in numerous vocal groups by 1956 and by the time The Mamas And The Papas had their first hit single in 1966 he would be thirty-one.

In the early Sixties he met a long-haired Californian beauty named Michelle Gilliam, whom he would later marry. She had a sweet voice, and so, together with a friend called Phil Blondheim (who would soon change his name to Scott McKenzie) they travelled the circuits as first The Journeymen and then The New Journeymen. After a minor nervous breakdown from Blondheim/McKenzie which culminated in him destroying his guitar on stage at Carnegie Hall he was edged out and Phillips met up with two Californian folkies called Denny Doherty and Cass Elliott. Doherty was a sure-footed vocalist who would eventually sing lead on several Mamas And Papas singles. Cass, or 'Mama' Cass as she was usually called, was a 20-stone kaftan-clad phenomenon with a heart made of such 18-carat gold that she had even married a casual boyfriend to enable him to dodge the draft for Vietnam.

In 1965 they practised singing together and, delighted with the results, began to travel and live as one big family. They all experimented with LSD and found it to their liking. Phillips became so dependent on it that at one stage he would not perform without it.

Barry McGuire, a fellow folkie who had had one of the biggest hits of that year with 'Eve Of Destruction', the anti-Vietnam song, advised them to see Lou Adler of Dunhill Records. They sang 'California Dreamin'' and 'Monday Monday', two of their future biggest hits, and secured a record contract. Soon an album came out.

All was not happy in the Mamas

And The Papas' camp however. The close personal lifestyle had inevitably led to some problems, not least the love affair that was brewing between Michelle Phillips and Denny Doherty. There was also a complex rivalry between Cass Elliott and Michelle Phillips based on the latter's good looks and the former's jealousy of same. Cass had charm, style and pizzazz but craved sexual attention, especially from Doherty. So there was a state of confusion as they faced up to stardom with the huge success of 'California Dreamin''.

Of course they were acclaimed in the press nationwide. Nobody had ever seen a group like this and their image – not that they'd planned it – was a magnet for newshounds. Not only did they look great, especially Michelle, they sounded great too. And fat girls the country over were identifying with the mighty free spirit that was Cass Elliott.

Their second single, 'Monday Monday', was just as successful as 'California Dreamin'' and they should have been in a position to reap the financial rewards. However, the turbulence in the group had reached such hostile levels that John Phillips presented the others with an ultimatum: either he went or Michelle did. It was no contest and, in the summer of 1966 Michelle was fired. She was soon replaced by a girl named Jill Gibson.

The remaining Mama and the two Papas went to London where they found that they were heroes of such luminaries as The Beatles and The Rolling Stones and suddenly they gained access to a world where everything had a chemical formula. Doherty preferred to drink but the other two dived in with both feet.

Back in America things did not work out with Gibson so late 1966 saw the return of Michelle to the group. Michelle and John Phillips set up home in Bel-Air and embarked on a drug binge that lasted throughout 1967.

Phillips it was who had the original idea for the Monterey Free Festival. Mulling over the possibilities of giving something back to the beautiful children of California he suddenly hit upon the idea of a weekend of pop music featuring such local talent as The Jefferson Airplane and Big Brother And The Holding Company, complemented by international artists like The Who and Ravi Shankar. The Mamas And The Papas would wind the whole thing up on the final day.

In order to publicize the event, he wrote a song about it which went, 'If you're going to San Francisco, be sure to wear some flowers in your hair'. He gave the song to his old friend Scott McKenzie to record and suddenly it was one of the best-selling records in the whole country. Not only had Phillips written one of the biggest hits of 1967, not only had he written the anthem for the Peace And Love generation, he has also written a song whose royalties would keep him in drugs for the next 13 years.

Phillips's role in the organization of

Monterey cannot be understated. With so many dazed hippies around, it was his administration that got the whole thing going smoothly, and he even had time to throw out a few unwanted acid dealers if their supplies did not meet the required standard.

But there was one major cloud on the horizon for 1967 – Cass had discovered heroin. She was restless to forge some sort of solo career, and the rest of the group were finding it difficult to record their new album. In addition, she was having extreme weight problems. All in all, she was floundering in a sea of losers and users. Towards the end of her career in the group she was arrested in Southampton when she disembarked from HMS *France* for the crime of stealing two blankets and a key from a hotel.

Ironically, the group was laden with dope at the time, but it was all academic since she was found not guilty.

The next Mamas And Papas single was released in 1968. However, to the chagrin of John Phillips, it was credited to Mama Cass alone, something about which he had not been consulted. However, he did not begrudge Cass her solo glory, and when she secured a week of performances at Caesar's Palace in Las Vegas there was a convoy of well-wishers there to see her. This was unfortunate, since she was so drug-addled that she could barely stand, and the show was a disaster.

Around this time Phillips met his future third wife, the woman who would share his Seventies hell, the South African actress Genevieve Waite. He also showed a lucky streak when he narrowly avoided being one of those butchered by the Manson family. He had heard of Manson from Dennis Wilson. Wilson, the drummer with the Beach Boys, had in the beginning enthused about Manson and his liberated young protégés, but later showed fear and loathing of the crazy messiah.

Phillips did not know much about the protégés, but he'd heard the songs of the messiah, and he thought they were appalling. However, for some reason, Roman Polanski suspected Phillips of being involved in the events that had led to the death of his wife, and only after a dramatic confrontation was Phillips's innocence assured.

With the break-up of The Mamas And The Papas came solo albums. *Wolf King of L.A.*, the first effort from Phillips, died in the shops, although he was still being praised in the music press as a vital songwriter. With the failure of the record he turned to cocaine and blanked out a little of the hurt.

By 1972, when Phillips married Genevieve Waite, it had been four years since his last hit record. But the list of wedding guests proved that he was now on a plane of celebrity status where hit records don't much matter and where nobody has to prove themselves. The Jaggers, Warren Beatty, Jack Nicholson, they all kept

John Phillips living in the jet set lounge.

By now his children from previous marriages were on drugs, although both of them were still in their early teens. A flirtation with LSD gave way to a dependency on cocaine, and there was enough of it lying around the house for the kids to dip in unnoticed once in a while. Phillips himself had reached the stage where the needle does the damage.

Not even the death of Cass Elliott shocked him back to sobriety. She died in London in July 1974, after a triumphant show at the Palladium. The story that has circulated ever since is that she choked to death on a ham sandwich. Phillips later put the death down to a heroin overdose. The truth seems much more mundane. She was just too fat, and her heart gave out.

John Phillips was now mainlining heroin, shooting it straight into his veins. He had a new circle of friends, all of whom were doing exactly the same as he was. And he spent a lot of time at the London home of Keith Richards and Anita Pallenberg.

Despite the crippling effects of heroin on the creative juices Phillips still had plans to record. An album produced by Mick Jagger was mooted, but eventually the sessions descended into full-scale mayhem when Phillips refused to come out of the bathroom to sing. One day he woke up and found he did not have any veins left.

A visit to a doctor seemed to provide the answer when the medical man assured him that cocaine could cure heroin addiction if one took enough of it. But all that happened was that Phillips became addicted to that too. He was now sticking a syringe into his hand every ten minutes.

His family fell apart. His son was a heroin addict and his daughter, a successful TV actress on American networks, was arrested for possession. The network suspended her and she was forced to enter a drug-rehabilitation programme.

Phillips himself was busted in 1980. It was serious., Not only was he in possession of drugs himself, but he was accused of dealing to others. He faced a colossal forty-five years in jail if found guilty. He had only one option – to try to preach the gospel to the TV cameras and hope for leniency from the court. Therefore, he and his daughter went on anti-drug crusades for most of the following year and dealt with the inevitable jeers from cynical journalists that it was about time. Occasionally he would be given a standing ovation when he told his harrowing story, most especially if the narrative was punctuated with the odd glimpse of his scarred hands.

It looked bad. Even Michelle was against him, telling tales of drunkenness and cruelty. That, and the fact that the only obvious recourse for someone who has survived cocaine and heroin cross-addiction is to become a raving alcoholic, cast a shadow over the proceedings.

Incredibly, John Phillips was jailed

for only 30 days and fined $15,000, a verdict that some resentfully attributed to his celebrity role.

He then put into action a new, though hardly improved, Mamas And Papas. The line-up was Phillips, Denny Doherty (who had had lingering problems with alcohol), Spanky McFarlane (a Cass semi-lookalike) and Phillips's daughter Laura McKenzie Phillips filling the Michelle role.

Michelle for her part was not overwhelmed by the volte face. 'I just hope John's ninth detoxification attempt is more successful than his previous eight,' she wrote to one magazine.

# Florence Ballard

In the whole catalogue of sidewinding, double-bluffing, hard bargaining and back-stabbing that constituted the seamier, less publicized side of the swinging Sixties, there is perhaps nothing quite so shameful as the treatment meted out to Florence 'Blondie' Ballard. Nobody stands accused here of any particularly heinous crimes – although the stone-bleeding business deals of her record company Tamla Motown did not exactly help her when she found herself sacked and alone at the end of 1967. And nobody is arguing that she was too dumb to stick up for herself and got taken for a major ride. The stitch-up, when it came, was a slow, subtle turnaround. And all of a sudden Florence Ballard, the supreme Supreme, the one with the best voice, the most attractive looks and personality, the band's founder, discovered that while the decade continued to sparkle for those around her, she was struggling to pay for her kids' meals.

Certainly the nine years she spent with The Supremes do not seem to have been the non-stop party that they were for Diana Ross. Phased out by the powerful Motown axis of Ross and her alleged lover/mentor Berry Gordy Jr, she slid slowly to the bottom of the heap and died a truly tragic figure. Possibly the saddest thing about her death is that it took place in exactly the same surroundings that she had dreamed of – and succeeded in – leaving. The money she made was gone, the jewellery pawned, the house sold, the dream poisoned and over.

Although Ms Ross tells it differently, Florence Ballard was the original leader of The Supremes. This was before they were even called The Supremes, when they were The Primettes, pre-Berry Gordy, unaware of the mighty Motown conveyor belt that was to slide hit after hit into the teenage jukeboxes. And it was long before *Diane* Ross announced in front of the other two Supremes that her real name was Diana and she would refuse to answer to anything else.

Originally there were four Primettes

– Diane Ross, Florence Ballard, a slightly older girl named Betty McGlown and Mary Wilson, who was to be the only remaining Supreme at the group's disintegration in the late Seventies. Ballard had got them their chance, which had arisen when the manager of a local Detroit male vocal group, The Primes, saw an opening for a 'sister' group. She was the lead singer.

Ballard was the eighth of 13 children, raised in a cramped ghetto in Detroit. Her family had moved there from the rural South so that her father could get work in Motor City. Florence exhibited an inherited brashness, a charming exterior which made her the inevitable focal point of The Primettes.

They secured something of a reputation in their own area as a first rate vocal harmony group, and everyone who saw them agreed that they had a superb, passionate lead singer.

Around this time Florence Ballard was brutally raped by a young man who tempted her into his car. Devastated by the incident itself, and the hell of reliving it when the case came to court, Ballard considered giving up singing. In the end she stuck with The Primettes, although friends noticed the difference. 'After that there was no laughter, no fun left in her,' said one.

Linking up with shrewd local record producer Berry Gordy Jr, they changed their name at his insistence to The Supremes. Betty McGlown had left so the remaining three – Ballard, Wilson and Ross – perfected their act, became close friends and waited for the hits to come.

They didn't, not at first. A string of totally forgettable releases left them dejected and unprepared for Gordy's brainwave: for the next record, he decreed, Diane Ross would sing lead vocals. At the time it seemed little more than a quirk. After all, nobody who ever heard them would seriously suggest that Ross was a better singer. But Wilson and Ballard would never sing lead, either of them, on a Supremes single again while Ross was in the group.

And when the hit *did* come, in 1964 with 'Where Did Our Love Go', the formula had been indelibly inscribed in black plastic. The role of Florence Ballard in the group would henceforth be little more than a cameo.

The Motown operation left nothing to chance. The Supremes were groomed for stardom; they went to charm school to learn about poise and deportment, and were instructed on how to treat their breathless young male fans. In addition, various false attachments were recommended to beef up the waif-like figures of Ross and Wilson. After a knockout appearance on the phenomenally influential Ed Sullivan Show, they became the hot buttered toast of America.

To the initial amusement of the other two, Ross began to date Gordy. She had been his secretary for a spell and been involved in administration duties concerning the group, and this put her in an undeniably strong position. The others noticed unpleasant changes in her personality. She was insisting on special privileges; she was making sure to dress differently from them; she was throwing superstar tantrums. It all came to a surprising head during a routine magazine interview when she announced that she was in fact *Diana* Ross, and could people kindly make a note of this for future reference?

Shortly afterwards, Florence Ballard's crowd-pleasing solo spot, a highly individual version of 'People' from the film *Funny Girl*, was axed from the show, never to return.

There was an obvious clash in personalities now. Ballard and Wilson were perfectly happy to socialize with fans, even giving them cash if they looked like they needed it badly. According to Wilson's autobiography, Ross became remote and downright dismissive of her audience. Encouraged by Gordy, she acted so much like a star that eventually they gave her the star dressing room.

Not only was Ross beaming in on personal stardom, she had to be observed doing it. So she took to walking ahead of Ballard and Wilson when entering a room, taking the applause on behalf of The Supremes and on behalf of herself. She was already handling all the interviews, which were inevitably published with the word 'Leader' affixed to Ross's name.

Florence Ballard began to drink heavily, missing the occasional press conference. She figured, not unreasonably, that since Ross was liable to answer all her questions for her what was the point of being there? However, Gordy took a dim view of this intransigence and her affair with Thomas Chapman, latterly Gordy's humble chauffeur, displeased him still further. Crucially, she was putting on a lot of weight, something about which Ross was not noticeably reticent.

The subtle strokes became outright hammer blows, and The Supremes underwent another name change. This time they became Diana Ross And The Supremes and by now Florence Ballard did not care whether she sang or stayed at home. Gordy and Ross contrived to have her squeezed out of the group in July 1967, and she was replaced by former Patti LaBelle backing singer Cindy Birdsong. The official reason for the split was Ballard's 'exhaustion'.

Post-Supremes she married Chapman, later bearing him three children. She signed a recording deal with ABC, but nothing successful came of it. Chapman's attempts to manage her career back to stardom failed disastrously and she foundered in sleazy bars and tacky clubs. At a would-be get-together to clear the air with the Motown people she was repeatedly humiliated by Ross and left in a drunken, embittered rage. She never forgot this.

Ross herself left the group in January 1970 and embarked on an awesomely successful solo career. Among other triumphs she received an Oscar nomination for her portrayal of the doomed singer Billie Holiday in the film *Lady Sings The Blues*. Mary Wilson kept The Supremes going until the eventual schism in 1977, although habitués of cabaret establishments are occasionally privy to some sort of reformation.

Ballard, meanwhile, sank into an overweight, poverty-stricken nightmare. Her attempt to sue Gordy for more money, money which she felt she had been cheated out of, was laughed out of court, and she was forced to pawn the jewellery her success had bought her. She split with her husband and sold her house. Even after its sale she used to return there, sometimes with her children in tow, and observe its changes from the opposite side of the street. In 1975 she applied for Aid For Families With Dependent Children. When a local paper was tipped off about a possible human interest story about her the reporter found her trying to scrape enough money together to buy her children a head of cabbage. She had hit rock bottom.

It is a common misconception that she died at this miserable stage in her life. In actual fact, she came into a lot of money soon afterwards, although no-one is sure how. Friends claim that this encouraged her and that she made serious attempts to pull herself out of the alcoholic quagmire.

She never made it. In February 1976, after drastic efforts to lose weight had failed, she died of a heart attack brought on by a blood clot in a coronary artery.

At her funeral service Diana Ross asked to be allowed to make a brief, emotional tribute. As the procession filed slowy out of the church the organist played The Supremes' last hit – 'Someday We'll Be Together'. The irony of the choice was numbing. For, hounded by Ross and Gordy to take that last necessary step out of the spotlight, she had not even been allowed to sing on the record.

Fleetwood Mac

## Fleetwood Mac

1988 saw the venerable Fleetwood Mac, originally a British R&B band but now highly regarded practitioners of what is known as AOR (album-oriented rock, or sometimes adult-oriented), celebrating its 21st anniversary with a mega-selling album, *Tango In The Night*, which, like several of its predecessors, topped the album chart in various lands, including Britain.

The years since the group's triumphant emergence at the Windsor Jazz & Blues Festival in 1967, alongside a galaxy of star names including Eric Clapton (then in Cream), Jeff Beck, Rod Stewart and Ron Wood (all part of Beck's group), and one time Rolling Stone Mick Taylor, saw ups and downs, triumphs and tragedies on a scale which would almost appear too far-fetched to be believable – except that they were true.

The group was formed by Peter Greenbaum, a guitarist from London's

East End, who first found fame as replacement for Eric Clapton in John Mayall's Bluesbreakers. Calling himself Peter Green, the guitarist soon formed a bond with two other Bluesbreakers, drummer Mick Fleetwood and bass player John McVie, and with the addition of a young devotee of blues legend Elmore James named Jeremy Spencer, Fleetwood Mac Mark 1 was quickly a sensation. At first the band did not include McVie, who was hedging his bets and remaining with Mayall until Green could guarantee him a regular income. His position as bass player was temporarily filled by Bob Brunning, today Headmaster of an infants school in South London.

When McVie finally agreed to join, the group found success at speed. By the end of 1968, they had not only achieved a chart-topping hit with 'Albatross', but had also expanded to a quintet with the arrival of a third singer/guitarist, Danny Kirwan. Things went well for a while, with several more big hits such as 'Man Of The World' and 'Oh Well'. But Green was experiencing problems in dealing with the fame, and particularly the money, which stardom brought in its wake, and in May 1970 left the band. His replacement, Christine Perfect, was a singer and keyboard player, who had enjoyed some fame as vocalist on 'I'd Rather Go Blind', a hit for the group Chicken Shack, of which she was a member. In addition, she happened to be married to John McVie.

The hits soon stopped, and not long after Christine McVie joined, Fleetwood Mac found themselves without another founder member, when Jeremy Spencer disappeared during an American tour and resurfaced as a member of a religious cult known as the Children Of God. Green was persuaded to help the band fulfil their US touring commitments, but was adamant that this was just a temporary measure. In August, 1972, Kirwan was asked to leave the band – according to a surviving member of the band, Kirwan was a nervous wreck, which made attempts to restore the group to its former status extremely difficult. Each of the three singer/guitarists has recorded subsequently, but none of the resulting albums have achieved commercial success to compare with that of Fleetwood Mac's earlier days.

Someone claiming to be Jeremy Spencer turned up in London during the Seventies, and was booked into a large London concert hall. Bob Brunning had been asked to confirm the identity of the ersatz Spencer, which he did, later saying that the bogus Spencer seemed to know the answers to several searching questions which should have unmasked an impostor.

Green re-adopted the Jewish faith he had largely abandoned in favour of rock stardom. He was sufficiently troubled by substantial royalty payments relating to his compositions and recordings for Fleetwood Mac that he allegedly threatened an accountant with a gun in his desire to stop these payments. He subsequently spent time in a mental hospital. Kirwan periodically also finds life similarly difficult and is known to psychiatrists.

Between mid-1971 and the start of 1975, three more musicians joined and then left the band. The longest of the three to endure was the first American to join Fleetwood Mac, Bob Welch. The briefest stay was that of vocalist Dave Walker, who was asked to leave due to his having an affair with Mick Fleetwood's wife. The group's five albums during Welch's time with the band were at best minor successes, and then only in America, where the group were now based. Stateside audiences seemed more interested in Fleetwood Mac than their British counterparts, who clearly considered the group a pale imitation of the one which had scored with 'Albatross', 'Man Of The World' and so on.

Everything changed for the better when Lindsey Buckingham, a singer/guitarist/songwriter, and his then girlfriend, singer/songwriter Stephanie (Stevie) Nicks signed on when Welch departed. The first album by the new line up was simply titled *Fleetwood Mac*, and sold prodigiously around the world. Fleetwood Mac Mark 10 became the most successful line up thus far, and was in great demand, touring internationally for the best part of a year without a break. This unexpected activity placed an immense strain on the group's personal relationships, and the follow-up album, *Rumours*, featured a collection of songs detailing the events which led to the McVies' marriage breaking up and the end of the romantic relationship between Buckingham and Nicks.

Mick Fleetwood was at the time also experiencing marital traumas (no doubt in the wake of the Dave Walker incident), and he and his wife Jenny (sister of Patti Boyd, who has at various times been married to both George Harrison and Eric Clapton) also divorced. Subsequently, Fleetwood and Jenny remarried and re-divorced.

The personal anguish which each member of Fleetwood Mac must have been feeling as they entered the recording studio to make *Rumours* appears to have made no difference to the end product which became the biggest selling album ever. Although it probably no longer holds that title it has sold an estimated 20 million copies plus at the time of writing.

More recently, after the recording of *Tango In The Night*, Lindsey Buckingham has also left Fleetwood Mac, and two newcomers have joined the band. What fresh experiences may yet accrue to this ultimately durable group can only be guessed at.

# The Beach Boys

In 1988 Brian Wilson released his first solo album. If one didn't know anything about Wilson, this would not be of particular note. But to several generations of fans who continue to regard The Beach Boys as the epitome of sunshine music, it was an event akin to John Lennon's return to recording when it seemed that the ex-Beatle had abandoned music in favour of learning to bake bread.

Brian Wilson was the eldest of three brothers who formed the nucleus of The Beach Boys. He was the group's main songwriter, its musical heart, and his songs, arrangements, productions and clear vision had made the five-man group (completed by a cousin of the Wilsons, Mike Love, and a school friend, Al Jardine) the biggest American band during the Sixties, with classic hit after classic hit featuring in the charts. Success of this measure would be quite enough for any ordinary person, but Brian was not content to rest upon his laurels, despite the fact that his hearing in one ear was defective to the point where he was unable to listen stereophonically.

As records became more and more complex, and production values increased in sophistication, Wilson strove to keep up with the musical advances being pioneered by other artists, notably The Beatles. The difference was that the Lennon & McCartney songwriting team consisted of two equal parts, either of whom could write tunes or lyrics. With The Beach Boys, Brian was sometimes helped out with words by Mike Love, but wrote many of the group's classics by himself. The Beatles could rely on George Martin's skill as a producer and arranger, but Brian had to do all that by himself too, as well as performing live with the group on an endless round of concerts.

By the end of 1964, with a dozen US Top 40 hits to the group's credit, all masterminded by Brian, as well as seven hit albums which were largely his conception, Brian had a nervous breakdown during an Australian tour. He had recently married and almost simultaneously had experienced marijuana for the first time.

An early replacement for touring purposes was latterday country music star Glen Campbell. A permanent sixth Beach Boy, Bruce Johnston, joined the band after Campbell left to become 'the dream of the everyday housewife', to quote the title of one of his hits.

With the burden of live work lifted – apart from the mental anguish produced by overworking, the proximity to powerful amplification systems caused him hearing problems – Brian began work on the group's next album, *The Beach Boys Today*, and used the freedom from group commitments to experiment while they toured. At first this produced pop masterpieces like 'California Girls', and the album *Pet Sounds* was regarded as one of the finest albums of the Sixties. Three tracks from it, including 'Sloop John B' and the sublime 'God Only Knows' were big hits.

The only clouds on the horizon came with the release of *Sgt. Pepper* by The Beatles, which totally eclipsed *Pet Sounds* commercially. There was also growing resentment against Brian on the part of the rest of the group. Reportedly, he had virtually made the album on his own, multi-part vocals and all, while the group were out on the road, and it was presented to them as something of a fait accompli.

Brian may have sympathized with his group's wishes to be involved in the recordings rather than merely trying to copy the hit records which bore their name, but over which they had little influence. There was greater collaboration in the next song the group released. It would become the most familiar song associated with The Beach Boys – 'Good Vibrations'. An undoubted masterpiece, it involved other group members vocally, and Mike Love wrote the lyrics, although it was recorded over a six month period and is said to have cost $50,000 to record. It topped the charts on both sides of the Atlantic, and Brian had caught up with The Beatles again – at least, in his own mind.

He was experimenting with every imaginable drug, including acid (LSD), which may explain his massive overconfidence. The next album on which he embarked, *Smile*, is still legally unreleased 20 years after it was abandoned by Brian, although substantial portions of various stages of the album have escaped into the hands of bootleggers. Although its suppression has led to it becoming something of a legend, those who are familiar with the album are unimpressed, considering it totally lacking in direction.

Brian referred to it as 'writing a teenage symphony to God', and perhaps in an attempt to reach God-like mental status, he ingested vast quantities of drugs. His collaborator as lyricist for *Smile*, Van Dyke Parks, was a charmingly eccentric child actor turned composer whose first album, *Song Cycle*, was critically praised but commercially ignored.

One song from the *Smile* sessions that was completed and released as a single was 'Heroes & Villains', a musically complex item which was substantially less of a hit than 'Good Vibes'. The rest of the album had even less to recommend it. Finally, it was removed from the record label's schedule, although about half a million sleeves had been printed; these have been circulating ever since.

Brian Wilson had apparently drugged himself into oblivion by now. Stories were circulating about how he had a sandpit constructed in his living room. The grand piano being in the sandpit allowed Brian to wiggle his toes in the sand while he composed – until the Wilson family pets found the sand very useful as a bowel-evacuation station.

One of the tracks on *Smile* is known as 'Fire' (part of 'The Elements Suite'!). An army of string players who had assembled in a large recording studio were instructed by Brian, who had hired them, to don toy fire helmets. A bucket containing burning embers was brought into the studio at Brian's instigation – he said he wanted the musicians to smell smoke. It took over 20 attempts with all the string players before Brian left the studio with the track completed to his satisfaction. Later that day, he heard that a building near the studio where he had been working had burned down, and decided that this was not a coincidence – a journalist who witnessed 'Fire' being recorded said it evoked 'roaring, windstorm flames, falling timbers, mournful sirens and sweating firemen'.

Whether or not Brian's curious behaviour had a knock-on effect on the rest of the group is difficult to decide, but other Beach Boys also began to get involved in bizarre situations. The pop royalty of the period, including The Beatles, Mick Jagger and Marianne Faithfull, Donovan and others appeared to legitimize the celebrated Maharishi Mahesh Yogi by attending the latters' classes to learn about transcendental meditation. But most of them stopped quite quickly when they discovered that the Maharishi was just as worldly as they were and was interested other than spiritually in one of the female converts from the showbiz world. John Lennon apparently became

disenchanted when the 'guru' was unable to satisfactorily explain why Brian Epstein had suddenly died while The Beatles were meeting the Maharishi. Mike Love, however, was captivated by TM (even writing several forgettable songs about the subject) and has remained a disciple.

Dennis Wilson's involvement with mass killer Charles Manson was rather more dangerous than Love's belief in the Maharishi, and details of this episode can be found elsewhere in this book. Of the three Wilson brothers, Dennis was the one with the teenage heart-throb looks, plus an insatiable appetite for sex, and Manson's murderous crew included several attractive girls who would bestow their sexual favours liberally. While Mike Love's interest in TM was intellectual, Dennis's interest in Manson was sparked by lust for the latter's female followers, although he justified his friendship with Manson by claiming that the latter possessed immense songwriting talent.

At least it didn't cost The Beach Boys too much financially, which was more than could be said of the group's tour with the Maharishi, billed as 'The Most Exciting Event Of The Decade'. At the first gig of the tour at a huge New York auditorium, a witness noted that the police who were present to keep order outnumbered the audience. Even when a reasonable crowd paid to see The Beach Boys, they left in droves during the opening set by the 'guru', who tried to use the opportunity to make fresh converts to his so-called religious cause. The tour was cancelled halfway through, and lost around $500,000 and this was 20 years ago, when half a million was a vast amount to throw away.

Manson, while not being a drain on The Beach Boys as a whole, fleeced Dennis spectacularly over the period when they were 'friends', and this culminated in Manson threatening both Dennis and his son, Scott. As it happened, little resulted from the threats – Dennis would destroy himself without help from Charlie.

The majority of the records released by The Beach Boys since 'Heroes & Villains' had been musically forgettable and commercially disastrous. One possible exception was 'Surf's Up', a song written by Brian and Van Dyke Parks which was rescued from the *Smile* debacle and became the title track of a 1971 Beach Boys album. Other than that, Brian wasn't doing much apart from staying in bed, sometimes for weeks at a time. He was still ingesting copious quantities of drugs and had virtually given up writing songs – those that he did present to the group were fragmentary and useless as far as resurrecting the group's fast fading fame was concerned.

It was at this point that the decision was made that The Beach Boys should move from Los Angeles to Holland, to make a new album. No doubt the thinking was that not only would this distance Brian from his coterie of dubious drug-dealing friends, it would also restore Dennis to

some kind of normality, as his paranoia about the Manson gang, many of whom were still around LA, might lessen.

Eventually, over 30 people and several dogs moved to Amsterdam, although initially Brian was not among this multitude, which not only included the group members, but also their entire families and servants and various employees plus *their* families and servants. Brian twice got as far as the Los Angeles airport, but then insisted that he had forgotten something and missed the plane on both occasions. A third time, everyone thought he was on his flight, but when the plane touched down in Holland, Brian's seat was empty apart from his passport and ticket. He had made an excuse to get off the plane before departure and had fallen asleep in an airport lounge. He was put on the next plane.

The entourage was deployed in various hotels, then rented houses, around Amsterdam, and reportedly there was almost constant telephonic contact between one or other of the party in Amsterdam and numerous parties in the US. Then the group decided that instead of utilizing the perfectly adequate recording facilities in Holland, they would construct their own studio in a converted barn. Such a scheme was hardly the kind of thing you might attribute to Einstein, but that wasn't all. What was to happen was that a complete studio was to be assembled in a warehouse in LA, after which it would be dismantled and rebuilt in Holland after all the constituent parts had been air-freighted across the Atlantic. Goodness knows what the eventual cost was.

After eight months in Holland, the album, which was wittily titled *Holland*, was delivered to Warner Bros, to whom The Beach Boys were signed at this point. Warners rejected it, despite the inclusion in the proposed package of a fairytale written by Brian entitled 'Mount Vernon & Fairway' which was to be pressed as a separate 7 in single and included in the album package as a bonus. Warners didn't want a fairytale, they wanted a hit single, and they couldn't hear one anywhere on the album. Van Dyke Parks came to the rescue again, with a song he and Brian had written shortly before, 'Sail On Sailor', and Warners finally agreed to release the album. It was little more than a minor hit.

Things were deteriorating. Brian was still incapable of consistent and constructive work. Dennis, while violently arguing with his wife, punched a plate glass window and was so badly injured that he was unable to use the hand for drumming for over a year. With no real prospect of a new album in the foreseeable future, both Warner Bros and Capitol, for whom they had made the vast majority of their hits, decided to embark on reissue programmes.

Warners had little to choose from, so simply reissued five previously released albums. Capitol, with more possibilities at their disposal, opted for a hits compilation with the inspired title of *Endless Summer*, and it topped the US album chart in 1974 after being advertised on television.

While this continuing interest in The Beach Boys was very gratifying to Mike Love and extremely useful in restoring the group's flagging finances, for Brian it must have been heartbreaking to realize that the great American public were considerably more interested in his group's early work, and had been virtually ignoring his newer confections. Brian was still not working on the road with the group, nor was he contributing much to their new recordings. He stayed in bed and took drugs.

On Midsummer's Day of 1975 at Wembley Stadium in London, Elton John topped a strong bill which also included The Eagles, the highly rated guitarist Joe Walsh and his band, and The Beach Boys. When Mike Love led the group into an hour-long set of their greatest hits, hardly touching on anything bar familiar singles, the sun was starting to set after a most un-English day of glorious sunny weather.

The group was rapturously received, and the majority of the 72,000 members of the audience considered them the highlight of a great day. When Elton came on and tried to better their remarkable performance, he made what many considered an error of judgement. He had just released a brand new album, which he wished to promote, so a large portion of his set consisted of songs which most of the audience

didn't know. After lustily singing along with The Beach Boys while the sun kept everyone pleasantly warm, the crowd wanted the singing to continue. But they didn't know the tunes, let alone the words to Elton's new material, and his usually energetic performance must have been an anti-climax.

The following summer, a compilation album of most of the songs they played that day provided The Beach Boys with their first chart-topping album in Britain. This meant that The Beach Boys were forever condemned to play their old hits as opposed to their more recent output, a sad situation which continues today.

Every now and then, the announcement would be made that 'Brian Was Back', and that he would be as much involved with a new album as he had been on *Pet Sounds*. In fact, one album, *The Beach Boys Love You*, released in 1977, was almost a reversion to the days when Brian would write and record much of an album while the rest of the group were on tour, and it wasn't as bad as several of the intervening albums. Little made any difference to the public perception of The Beach Boys as perhaps the best oldies band in the world.

Brian was playing with the band again, and so was Dennis, while several hired gun session men doubled the size of the group onstage. Dennis was in poor shape, prematurely middle aged through booze, dope and frequent cheating on

his wives. His voice was a croak. His latest wife – and this was unbelievable – was Mike Love's illegitimate daughter, and he had fathered a child by her, but as with most of his official and unofficial lovers, he had fallen out with her, and they were living apart. He had had five previous wives by the age of 39, and supposedly had an affair with President Reagan's daughter as well. Just after Christmas 1983, Dennis went swimming in the sea and drowned.

Brian, meanwhile, had discovered a new father figure. He had ballooned in size despite the appointment of security staff whose job it was to keep him on the straight and narrow. The arrival of Dr Eugene Landy, a psychiatrist, has been of immense and probably life-saving significance for Brian Wilson, who now looks better than for most of the past quarter of a century. Landy is also credited on Brian's songs as co-writer, and is Executive Producer of almost every record on which Brian has played recently.

His staff keep Brian under surveillance 24 hours a day, which must be costing him a fortune, but the bottom line is that Brian looks good and is more active musically than at any time since *Pet Sounds*.

At this point, he isn't even playing with The Beach Boys, whose hit-packed concerts continue to make them a major live attraction all over the world. The Beach Boys haven't made a new album in three years, and there seems little prospect of such a thing in the foreseeable future, although they actually returned to the top of the US singles chart in late 1988 with a song from a film called *Cocktail* entitled 'Kokomo'.

Brian's album qualified as one of the longest awaited in rock 'n' roll history. Not because it took a long time to produce, but because he should have made it 20 years before, which in a way he had, although those records were credited to The Beach Boys. *Brian Wilson* is a cleverly planned album, with several of the tracks credited to 'Wilson/Landy'. There is one long track which sounds as though it has been rescued from the still unreleased *Smile*, and a couple of collaborations with hotshot hitmakers which are the most commercial things on the album. Sadly it dropped out of chart contention after a few weeks.

Brian came to England in September 1988, his visit coinciding with the convention of The Beach Boys Fan Club, whose fanzine, *Beach Boy Stomp*, had supported the group through thick and (mostly) thin for several years. With impressive initiative, two of *Stomp*'s leading lights had secretly contacted Dr Landy to ask whether Brian might attend the fan convention. He arrived and the audience of 250 Beach Boys disciples behaved as if the Second Coming had taken place in that church hall in Greenford, a West London suburb. He played three songs, accompanying himself on electric piano, and then sat on the stage behind a table while every member of the audience brought him something to autograph – albums, posters, anything. Attempts to engage him in meaningful conversation were mostly a failure, but he sat there for over an hour signing his name. The general consensus among those aware of Brian's precarious mental health was that Dr Landy must have thought that it would be good therapy for him, and it probably was.

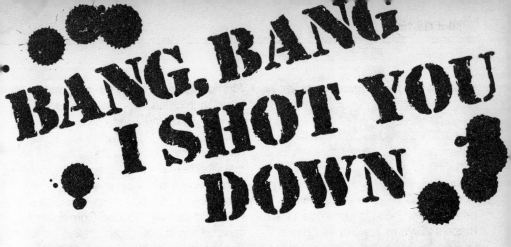

# BANG, BANG I SHOT YOU DOWN

## Charles Manson

It's a little known fact, but Charles Manson, the terrifying head honcho of the California devil children in the Sixties, has been in the charts. Of course, the people who bought the record were probably oblivious to Manson's influence. The song, 'Cease To Resist', is a fairly innocuous flipside to The Beach Boys' single 'Bluebirds Over The Mountain' – but the lyrics are all Manson's. The interesting thing is: with typical Mansonian slogan-wisdom he actually titled the song 'Cease To Exist'.

Before linking up with Dennis Wilson, Manson had made tentative forays into the music business. He was known as the writer and singer of heavy vibe songs, all about the universe and how we were heading for the apocalypse and how we were all men and all women were ours, or something like that. None of the producers of the period seemed too interested.

Manson had been in jail for most of his life by the time he tuned into The Beatles. A whole host of mystical reading matter and religious half-notions had slid him into cult hero overdrive even as early as 1963, and The Beatles convinced him that stardom was the answer. A fellow prisoner, one Phil Kaufman, was sufficiently impressed by Manson's songs to give him the names of some musical contacts when he was released.

A crucial element in the Manson story entered the ex-con's consciousness at this point. He took acid for the first time. His trip supposedly relived Jesus' agony on the cross. A few years later Manson would be scouring the Beatles' lyrics for directions, and calling himself Jesus Christ.

Manson kept the Beatle-watch going throughout the band's awesome creative phase 1966–67. He was sure that here were the messiahs of something bigger than just singing and playing guitars. This was youth power and glory, for ever and ever.

Charles Manson

Everything they did blew his mind. Even the dubious *Magical Mystery Tour*, a self-indulgent coach trip given artistic validity only by virtue of the fact that The Beatles were on board, gave him a cosmic hangover.

In early 1968 Manson formed a short-lived band, called The Milky Way. He played guitar and sang. They played a couple of local gigs but lack of audience enthusiasm precipitated their demise.

Then, in May of the same year, the Manson 'family' – a sprawling entourage of underage nymphettes and acid-crazed All-American boys – succeeded in finding some top-notch accommodation. They all piled into the home of Beach Boy Dennis Wilson. Wilson may not strictly have approved of the mass immigration; he certainly was not there to see it happen. But, faced with overwhelming nudity and sexual libertarianism on his return, he made an understandable lapse of judgement and made friends with them all.

Wilson was not, however, the coveted friend that Terry Melcher was. Melcher, the son of Doris Day, was another local resident. He was also one of the most sought-after producers in the country. His work on early Byrds singles had made him hugely successful, and Manson saw him as just the chap to get his struggling career finally off the ground. Melcher, unfortunately, was not overly impressed.

However, the music continued and Dennis Wilson was quoted as saying

that Charles Manson – whom he called the wizard – would quite likely record an album, which would be released on The Beach Boys' own label, Brother. In the final summer of sanity Manson did record, at Wilson's home recording studio. Shortly afterwards, distressed by the perpetual pilfering of Manson's family – gold records had been stolen and cars were changing hands without the owner's consent – Wilson threw Manson and his clan off the property. Manson replied by sending Wilson a bullet in the post, assuring him that there was another one like it for him.

Through lack of interest in his own songs, Manson began to loot Beatles songs for divine guidance and this policy reached the point of combustion in 1969 when *The Beatles* ('The White Album') hit the shops. This was the record that Manson later claimed had told him to kill.

There were four songs that basically inspired his warped gospel. 'Piggies', a socially-scathing George Harrison number detailing the base habits of the fat cats and obscenely rich; 'Rocky Racoon', which he interpreted astonishingly as a message of race hate; 'Blackbird', which compounded the philosophy of black versus white; and 'Helter Skelter'. 'Helter Skelter' is, admittedly, a shocking song, the most violent and disturbing Paul McCartney recording there is. Manson believed it was the band talking to him, telling him to get in touch. At one stage he actually did try to contact The Beatles.

Later in 1969 Manson began to

hassle Melcher insistently about producing him. Melcher kept asking for time to think. But time was running out. The original crimes of the family – theft, rape, drugs, extortion – had been horrific enough at times. Now Manson made it clear that he was prepared to murder all those who opposed him. He had reached personal insanity, and he had a terrifyingly faithful coterie of freaked-out kids only too eager to do the killing for him. Melcher's name was added to a possible death list. Incredibly, even the name of Tom Jones was once on Manson's death list.

The murders that Manson and his family committed throughout the autumn of 1969, incuding the slaughter of Sharon Tate, the rising film star who was carrying Roman Polanski's baby, had little to do with rock 'n' roll. Several rock stars, including John Phillips of The Mamas And The Papas, have claimed that but for the grace of God they would have been at the Tate household that night, enjoying the drugs and the soothing music.

The recordings that Manson made eventually surfaced on an LP, the cover of which was a reproduction of a *Life* magazine splash. The title was altered so that it read *Lie*. Manson looked somewhat less than human in the picture.

The producer, Phil Kaufman, later became something of a celebrity in the rock 'n' roll business. Calling himself an executive nanny and 'road mangler' (sic), he attached himself to The Rolling Stones on their '69 American tour. He became friends with Gram Parsons, a sad-voiced country cowboy and writer of sentimental songs who had been a Byrd for a while. Parsons made a couple of excellent coutry albums in the early Seventies before the extent of his rock 'n' roll lifestyle caught up with him in 1973 when he died of a suspected heroin overdose. In accordance with a mutual agreement, Kaufman hi-jacked the body from its resting place, got drunk as hell and burned the coffin containing his buddy's body.

# John and Yoko

When Mark Chapman assassinated – somehow the word 'murdered' does not suffice – John Lennon on December 8, 1980 he unwittingly set in motion a chain of events which culminated in 1988 with the publication of the latest in a series of scabrous, dirt-dishing, ruthlessly iconoclastic biographies by the

American writer Albert Goldman.

Goldman's study of Elvis Presley some years before had induced apoplexy in those Elvis fans who preferred to keep their memories pure. Not only was a highly damning portrait of a violent, incontinent drug fiend painted, it was done in such tones of cynical glee that the over-riding feeling was that Goldman denied Elvis any talent in the first place.

His work on John Lennon had been mooted as far back as 1984. The fears of Lennon fans, and of people who simply object to the relish with which books like this are invariably greeted, were justified. Lennon, it was noted in one review, was being murdered for the second time. Ironically, the week of the book's publication saw a deeply contentious film, Martin Scorsese's *Last Temptation Of Christ*, released to choruses of vitriol from practising Christians in America. Another hero was being maltreated, and his supporters did not appreciate it. Lennon's book was not boycotted, although Paul McCartney urged people not to buy it.

It is inevitable that in a life of 40 years, including countless parties and literally thousands of mentions in the press, John Lennon's name would be linked with drugs, sleaze, alcohol and violence. The fact that Goldman should feel honour-bound to inform us of this shows that he was not really paying attention to all the other Beatle books – the Fab Four were living it up, and down and sideways, as far back as 1960 in Hamburg. There seems no reason why John Lennon should *not* spend the greater part of the late Seventies in a lazy haze, worn out by too many trips on the Ferris Wheel, fed up with fame, music and people. The miracle is that in 1980 he decided that he wanted to re-enter the market place.

Up until *Double Fantasy*, the album

he made that year, his career post-Beatles had been mercurial. He had actually started making solo albums before the Beatles officially broke up, much to their displeasure. His first one, a joint effort with Yoko Ono, was entitled *Two Virgins*. As a record it was an astounding flop, consisting of the same sort of meandering electronic doodling that permeated 'Revolution 9' on The Beatles' 'White Album'. Yoko's role in the proceedings was unclear. However, the controversy lay with the sleeve, which featured John and Yoko totally naked, in a full-frontal shot. On the reverse, surprisingly enough, was a shot of their behinds.

On its completion in 1968 the other Beatles expressed their horror. For a start, the 'White Album' was due for release the same year, and they did not wants its place usurped by this inconsequential, needlessly provocative oddity. Lennon was persuaded to shelve it until November of 1968, by which time the 'White Album' was safely in the stores. When *Two Virgins* followed it, it did so in a paper bag with a tiny shot of Lennon's and Yoko's head. It sold miserably, possibly due to poor distribution.

The month before its release, John Lennon had experienced his first drugs raid at his home in London. This was an ominous change in fortune for the Beatles and for Lennon himself, a hint that the Seventies would see the police being a lot less lenient to the band than the Sixties had. Until then The Rolling Stones had been viewed by those in authority as the real threat while The Beatles were more of a mischievous national asset. When the situation changed, it did so with a vengeance. Forty police officers turned up to arrest the waif-like twosome of Lennon and Yoko. Even the House Of Commons thought that a little extreme. There was also speculation as to why two national newspapers had their cameras pointed before the police even showed up.

When the case came to court Lennon pleaded guilty in a gallant gesture to spare the pregnant Yoko. His guilty plea would later be used as an excuse to deny him American right of residence.

And Yoko had a miscarriage.

In March 1969 Lennon married Yoko in Gibraltar ('near Spain', as he put it in 'The Ballad Of John And Yoko') and they honeymooned in the Amsterdam Hilton. 'We're happy to be called a couple of freaks,' they announced, 'as long as we are happy and can make other people happy.' To make the honeymoon complete, they invited the world's press to photograph them in bed together. This was called a Bed-In. Or, sometimes, Hair Peace. Hair Peace was a travelling roadshow in the spring of 1969, as John and Yoko had much-publicized Bed-Ins in various capital cities. There was a prevailing feeling that the two of them had gone slightly off the rails.

Another album they released at this stage seemed to confirm this. *Unfinished Music No. 2: Life With The Lions* appeared to be nothing more than a vocal history of Yoko's miscarriage. Their next album, that same year, was called *The Wedding Album* and consisted mainly of John repeating the word 'Yoko' over and over, while Yoko returned the compliment. It was all very strange.

The Hair Peace concept – which remained throughout a vague, badly-defined idea – got even sillier. Acorns were planted in solemn ceremonies; billboard space was purchased to house huge 'War Is Over If You Want It' signs; and, in a hilarious gesture at a London gig featuring Lennon's new outfit The Plastic Ono Band, Yoko entertained the audience by handing an empty box to someone in the front row, telling him, 'There are plenty for everyone. Take one.' The box was labelled 'Smiles'.

The most ambiguous gesture made by Lennon during this period was to hand back the MBE which he had been awarded in 1966 with the other Beatles. In a note to The Queen he informed her that this was in protest against the British involvement in the Nigeria-Biafra war, against its support of America in Vietnam and 'against "Cold Turkey" (his new single) slipping down the charts'. He signed it, 'With love, John Lennon of Bag'. Bag Peace was the new gimmick. It involved lying in a bag. For peace.

'Cold Turkey' had been written about his efforts to kick heroin, which he had begun to take when The Beatles scene got heavy. It was a frightening song, one of his best, and its harsh shrieks of pain would be echoed just over a year later with his Primal Therapy album, *John Lennon/ Plastic Ono Band*.

For the moment he contented himself with having his penis filmed in various stages of erection for Yoko Ono's provocative movie, *Erection*. In an exciting follow-up, *Number Five*, she filmed his face, concentrating on his mouth, and slowed the film down so that every time he moved his lips the audience in the cinema where it played gave a spontaneous cheer.

She announced her ambition to make a film featuring the smiling face of 'every single human being in the world'. Asked about it later, she admitted there had been 'technical difficulties'. The couple saw out 1969 by getting involved in plans for a religious rock musical based on the life of Jesus Christ. Lennon eventually refused to play the title role unless Yoko was allowed to be Mary Magdalene. Tim Rice and Andrew Lloyd Webber probably never looked back.

Lennon's behaviour throughout this period is particularly surprising given that he was always the first to prick any balloons of pretentiousness that drifted in on the Beatles' horizon. When the Maharishi Mahesh Yogi came on the scene and invited them down to Wales he was the one who tumbled that the grizzly sage was · showing a less than spiritual interest in a female disciple. Hearing the telephone ring one afternoon the Maharishi wondered aloud who it could be. 'You're the bloody prophet,'

replied Lennon. 'You tell us.'

Lennon later wrote a song about the trip entitled 'Sexy Sadie', scolding the protagonist, 'you made a fool of everyone', and warning him/her, 'you'll get yours yet, however big you think you are'. The consensus among cynical Lennon-watchers was that Yoko was the Maharishi in malevolent female form and that this time Lennon was being, to adopt the honest vernacular, 'strung up like a kipper'.

1970 was the year of Janov. Dr Arthur Janov's book *The Primal Scream* has become essential reading for neurotic students everywhere, with its grim diagnoses of childhood repression and parental fear. The English group Tears For Fears took their name from one of his theories which recommended crying rather than bottling up worries.

John Lennon and Yoko underwent four months of intensive therapy, from June to September 1970, and in October Lennon returned to the studio to put the Janov ideas into the grooves of his new album.

The harrowing result, *John Lennon/ Plastic Ono Band*, was released in 1971 and stands as one of his best ever records. The first track, 'Mother', featuring a chillingly basic drum pattern from Ringo Starr, dealt with the two personal traumas of Lennon's youth – witnessing the death of his mother and seeing his father desert the family. The song ends in a crescendo of primal screams: 'Mama don't go/Daddy come home'.

It was similarly tense on other

tracks, notably the lengthy 'God', on which he listed all the things he didn't believe in, including The Beatles. The album finished with a lo-fi recording of Lennon singing 'My Mummy's Dead', in the tentative, disbelieving voice of someone who has just heard of it.

Everything suggested that perhaps Lennon's dalliance with the distractions of Hair Peace and Yoko's cinema had been momentary aberrations. Still, one credit on the album, attributing 'wind' to Yoko Ono, stumped people who could not hear flutes on any of the songs. Lennon was quick to explain. 'She played atmosphere', he assured his fans.

His next album, *Imagine*, was released in 1971. The first thing critics noticed was a song called 'How Do You Sleep' which appeared to be a damning indictment of Paul McCartney. The end of The Beatles had been an acrimonious one, as Lennon and McCartney ridiculed each other's songs and hurried to make solo albums. But the venom of 'How Do You Sleep' took everyone by surprise, especially the line, 'Those freaks was right when they said/That you was dead'. McCartney later replied on his best-selling album *Band On The Run* with his song 'Let Me Roll It'. However, it lacked the sheer brutality of Lennon's tongue ('The sound you make is muzak to my ears' indeed!)

Lennon's much-publicized retirement in 1974, after three more albums, coincided with his separation from Yoko. He took up with his secretary, May Pang, and formed a terrifying trio of carousers with singer Harry Nilsson and Keith Moon. No music was played – none of them was sober for long enough – but much merriment was had, although Lennon's enforced exit from Los Angeles' Troubador Club for wearing a sanitary towel round his head depressed those who hoped to see him in a recording studio again.

Re-united with Yoko, with a young son Sean and – at last – his American green card, Lennon claimed to be happier than ever. His retirement into what he called 'househusbandry' had made him fat and indolent perhaps, but there was no denying the charm of his comeback album *Double Fantasy*. Actually, it was a joint effort, divided song-wise down the middle, but it's Lennon's songs that people remember. One of them, 'Woman', would be a posthumous number one single in Britain.

December 8, 1980, had been a busy day in the studio for the Lennons. They had been putting the finishing touches to a new Yoko song called 'Walking On Thin Ice'. Returning home towards midnight to their New York apartment block they were confronted by a young man named Mark David Chapman who called out Lennon's name, and then fired several shots into his turning body. He then put away his gun and stood reading a copy of J. D. Salinger's novel *The Catcher In The Rye* while John Lennon bled to death. He later pleaded guilty to murder and was sentenced to life imprisonment.

A copy of the *Double Fantasy* album

was discovered by a fan propped up against the wall of the building. It transpired that this was Mark Chapman's personal copy, signed a few days previously by Lennon himself. Chapman expressed a wish from his prison cell that the record be auctioned off and the money donated to the gun control lobby in America.

Since Lennon's death a surfeit of inferior recorded material has emerged, each purporting to be positively the last work he ever made. It is irritating to listen to the half-finished ideas and nowhere-bound conversations on these records, especially since their release was not envisaged by the man who made them. Somehow they make him seem like a shoddy saint, being worshipped only until a better one comes along.

Goldman's biography took a sizeable hatchet to a few of the myths – alleging heroin abuse during the Seventies, especially by Yoko – but fortunately it is a truism that the myths outlive the truth. Somewhere out there in rock 'n' roll fantasy land there are people who still believe, even after all the laughter and the denials, that Paul McCartney is dead. There are noticeably more who refuse to accept such a tragic blow happening to their hero John Lennon.

# Sam Cooke

Sam Cooke's death in 1964 was one of the most violent ever suffered by a musician or singer, and was completely and tragically at odds with the gentle soulful strains of his music.

He sang melodic gospel-tinged songs for black audiences and for them he was a hero just as daunting and just as real as Elvis was for the whites. His hit songs – 'You Send Me', 'Wonderful World', 'Cupid' to name just three – perfected the style of commercial soul music. The fact that it worked spectacularly must have been a decisive factor in Berry Gordy crank-starting the Motown operation. Later singers, including Otis Redding, testified to Cooke's influence and his singles still send a lucrative shiver down the public's spine even today.

The sheer enormity of his influence suggested that his death might not have been an accident. The bizarre circumstances which led to it would seem to lend support to this argument. There are so many unanswered questions regarding the Cooke shooting that a conspiracy theory is almost inevitable.

Cooke had married his childhood sweetheart and was known as a clean-living family man. So it was almost incredible to hear of his being shot while trying to rape a girl he had picked up at a party. Evidently he had persuaded this girl, Elisa Boyer, to get into his car, saying that he would give her a lift home. Instead he drove to a Los Angeles motel and, although she says she was forced into going, she seems to have stood silenty by his side while he signed the register, 'Mr and Mrs Cooke'. She says that she then demanded to be taken home but, after Cooke assured her that he merely wanted to talk for a while, she followed him to the room. There he tried to undress her and she resisted. Fears that he would try to rape her made her snatch up her clothes as well as Cooke's and dash across to the motel office. Once inside she found a phone and called the police.

Cooke followed her to the office and began pounding on the door, demanding to talk to her. The motel manageress, a certain Mrs Franklin, told him that Elisa Boyer was not there. Cooke appeared to believe her and got in his car to drive away. But then he returned and resumed pounding. Mrs Franklin testified that Cooke then broke down the office door in a state of rage and proceeded to attack her. She managed to fight him off and get hold of a pistol, with which she shot him three times in the chest and abdomen. He did not die at once.

Instead he leapt at her in an even greater rage whereupon she struck him with a stick. The stick broke but she kept hitting until he lay still. When the police eventually arrived he was dead.

Hearing this evidence, the inquest court ruled that the killing was justifiable homicide. Nevertheless the questions will not answer themselves. In an effort to find out what really happened that night Cooke's manager later hired a private detective to work it all out. He never came up with any satisfactory conclusions.

Sam Cooke's funeral was a tempestuous affair, with almost 200,000 people turning up to pay their respects. Many of them were hysterical, most were crying. Hundreds were crushed in the desperate attempt to take a look at his body for the last time and the local Chicago press ran stories on the pandemonium.

A week later another 5,000 people attended a funeral service for the dead singer in Los Angeles.

# Acknowledgements

The Publishers wish to thank
the following photographers and agencies:

LFI, pages 78–9, 85, 95, 115, 127;
LFI/Janet Macoska, pages 6, 47;
LFI/Chris Walter, page 57;
Rex Features, pages 12, 33, 39, 43, 66–7, 139, 150;
Frank Spooner Pictures, page 110;
Syndication International, pages 21, 73, 101;
and Topham Picture Library, page 123.